# THE DIVORCE PUZZLE

## CONNECTING THE PIECES
## COLLABORATIVELY

AN ANTHOLOGY
EDITED BY JORYN JENKINS

This work is based, in part, on actual clients of the authors. Names and identifying details have been changed to protect the privacy of the persons involved. This publication is designed to provide accurate and authoritative information with regard to its subject matter. It is sold with the understanding that the publisher is not engaged in rendering legal, accounting, or other advice. If legal advice or other expert assistance is required, seek the services of a competent professional. The opinions expressed by this book's authors are not endorsed by Open Palm Press or Joryn Jenkins and are the sole responsibility of the authors. Because of the Internet's dynamic nature, any Web addresses or links referenced herein may have changed since publication and may no longer be valid.

Although the authors and publisher have made every effort to ensure that the information in this book was correct at press time, they do not assume and hereby disclaim any liability to any party for any loss, damage, or disruption caused by errors or omissions, whether such errors or omissions result from negligence, accident, or any other cause.

This title is available at special quantity discounts for bulk purchases for sales promotions, premiums, fundraising, and educational use. Special versions or excerpts can also be created to fit specific needs. Visit us online at www.OpenPalmPress.com.

# TABLE OF CONTENTS

# INTRODUCTION

The collaborative divorce process is a means to an end, the end being a final judgment of divorce. These days, a couple can take any of many roads to that destination, mediation, litigation, and cooperation being but a few, but the most holistic is collaboration.

The collaborative approach to negotiating a divorce agreement requires just one thing, that the spouses each retain an attorney who signs an agreement to be disqualified from representing his client in court. This disqualification arrangement frees the lawyers to focus their time and talents solely on enabling their clients to reach a marital settlement agreement that they design, with the help of the collaborative team. No longer are the lawyers required to spend their time and energy, not only negotiating a settlement, but also preparing for trial.

But the collaborative divorce process often employs more than just two attorneys. The interdisciplinary team of professionals can include any number of players: always the two lawyers, of course, but often a financial neutral, who might be a certified public accountant, a financial planner, a certified divorce financial advisor, or perhaps some other financial expert, and often a mental health professional, a psychologist, a licensed mental health counselor, a licensed marital and family therapist, or a professional with similar credentials.

This collaborative mental health professional can perform any number of functions and can serve in any number of roles. The "coach," as she is often called, provides an invaluable service to the collaborative divorce team. She offers a specific skill set that is intrinsic to establishing an atmosphere of cooperation, reasonableness, and respect. She often runs the meetings, is the keeper of time, is responsible for keeping the team on track, and helps to maximize the process and outcomes.

Throughout the process, she is likely to assist the clients in their negotiations and may well mentor them in employing problem-solving and effective communication skills. She will help each client verbalize his thoughts, feelings, and requests, and she will help the other client to "hear" him and to understand those requests. She "coaches" each client to better present and listen to the ideas being shared by his counterpart.

This professional may also employ various strategies to enhance the other collaborative team members' effectiveness.

If there are children involved, she will likely assist the clients in recognizing and coordinating their respective parenting styles to enhance their future co-parenting relationship. If a child specialist is not a member of the team, the coach will help the clients formulate their parenting plan.

Regardless of whether there are children involved, the coach plays a crucial role because she assists the clients in achieving acceptable outcomes, taking into consideration their expressed goals, interests, and concerns. Because the coach is trained in human behavior, communication skills, personalities, etc., she is more able than the other professionals to defuse destructive situations and prevent progress-halting situations. Although she is often a therapist in other settings, rather than providing therapy, her role is to coach the clients, the team, and the process.

When one explains the roles of the various professionals who might serve on the collaborative team to a potential client, many clients respond, "I don't need a mental health professional. I don't need therapy. I'm not crazy." But, in the collaborative process, the mental health practitioner facilitates the process, rather than providing therapy, sending clients to treatment, or making diagnoses. In fact, if therapy *is* necessary, the coach must refer the client to another mental health professional because she can't wear her therapist hat while acting on a collaborative team. Instead, her role is to keep the clients in line and focused on their true goals and interests.

In many communities, the coach is the leader of the full team meetings. Having insight into the clients' relationship, as well as specialized training in the human psyche, the coach is in a better position than the other professionals to relate to the clients and to ensure they feel comfortable and heard. And she gives guidance to everyone involved.

Collaborative practice is still evolving. Some communities utilize a one-neutral-coach model and others use a model with two aligned coaches. Generally, communities have their own protocols regarding which model is most often used, however, certain couples may require their team to deviate from the standard community model to meet their specific needs.

The two models are fundamentally different. Those who prefer the one-coach model argue that two allied coaches render the process adversarial. A one-coach model may save costs and not be as intimidating because it reduces the number of professionals that clients must retain.

However, those who utilize the two-coach model believe that it is important for each client to feel that he has someone on his side to support his goals and interests. In certain cases, especially those implicating mental health, substance abuse, or domestic violence issues, a two-coach model may be more effective. The role of the aligned coach in the two-coach model is to be there for his client, to focus on emotional, therapeutic changes within his client, to coach his client through the process, and to work in conjunction with the other client and her coach.

In communities utilizing the aligned coach model, the financial professional functions as the neutral facilitator at the meeting, guiding the team through the process.

## A BRIEF HISTORY

When the collaborative divorce process was initially developed, many newly trained collaborative attorneys did not understand the role of the collaborative mental health professional. After all, their clients didn't need therapy; they just wanted a divorce! Thus, when collaborative divorce became interdisciplinary early in its evolution, the different disciplines still trained separately. There may have been one unified session at a training, but then each discipline would separate into breakout sessions.

Initially, early practice groups were only open to attorneys. If coaches were included, it was only on an ancillary basis. In fact, attorneys often used the coach on a collaborative team on an as-needed basis, sometimes adding them in the midst of the process after matters had escalated to an unmanageable level, if they utilized them at all.

In the years since coaches were first introduced into the process, it has become evident that to obtain the greatest benefit from collaboration, a coach should be part of the team from the start.

Aligned coaches provide direct support for their clients, who are often fragile and stressed. Neutral coaches facilitate the process, removing the positional sense brought by the attorneys and enabling the lawyers to collaborate together.

Beyond defining goals and interests, the coach's role is to observe all participants and their reactions, read body language, actively listen to participants, notice when team members are becoming upset, call breaks when appropriate, confer privately with team members to diffuse heated situations, and ensure that participants remain mindful to the process.

Eventually, attorneys realized what an asset the mental health practitioner was to the collaborative team. They began to welcome them into their practice groups. Trainings became truly interdisciplinary. Utilizing a mental health practitioner on the team is fast becoming the norm, rather than the exception.

Now, as the collaborative approach to *civil* dispute resolution begins to make itself known, the same questions arise. Why add a mental health practitioner to the resolution team if this professional brings little to the table other than an added expense? This will be one of the questions explored at the 13th Annual Meeting of the Global Collaborative Law Council in Tampa, Florida, in September 2017.

### SO WHAT'S IN A NAME? EVERYTHING.

Former President of the International Academy of Collaborative Professionals (IACP) and co-author (with Stu Webb) of *The Collaborative Way to Divorce*, Ron Ousky has commented on the fact that collaborative professionals around the country have differing ideas about which professionals should be included on a "full team." He adheres to Stu Webb's collaborative paradigm, which requires only that attorneys agree to withdraw if matters proceed to court.

Ron's guiding principles require that professionals "stay fully client centered . . . open to creative 'value added' methods to get the help of more professionals with less cost," and that community practices should be "influenced significantly by the cultural and demographic needs of that community." He advises:

> Growth of Collaborative Practice will be enhanced by obtaining clarity and simplicity about our model and the definition of Collaborative Practice . . . . This clarity is important to help our community unify "our brand" and will avoid the divisiveness caused by the ongoing development of other aspects of the model. The best ideas may still be ahead of us. If we stay true to our basic definition of Collaborative Practice, we will allow Collaborative Practice to stay client centered and we will encourage the continued development of great ideas.[1]

Throughout our various collaborative communities, we refer to the coach by many titles: coach, collaborative divorce coach, CDC, aligned coach, neutral, mental health professional, MHP, facilitator, family specialist, child specialist, and communications specialist. Obviously, this can be very confusing to the layperson, as well as to those professionals new to collaborative practice. For this reason, we must standardize the term we use for the collaborative mental health professionals so that we use the same term worldwide.

It is incumbent upon us to choose one simple term that applies to all collaborative mental health professionals so laypeople feel comfortable and know who that person is, what his role is, and of what he is capable. As Stu Webb reminded me in an e-mail earlier today, clear branding is critical to marketing the collaborative process, and if we don't settle on one term to define this unique role, it will be more difficult for us to market the collaborative concept.

Whichever term is used must be universally used amongst collaborative professionals.

Despite the role being titled differently in different parts of the world, they all fall under the ethical and role definitions set by IACP, and they all have commonalities. For this reason and for the sake of consistency, clarity, and reference to the IACP standards, we use the term "coach" throughout this book.

The IACP now uses the term "collaborative divorce coach" or "CDC." This term was originally coined by collaborative innovators Dr. Peggy Thompson and Nancy Ross, LCSW in the mid-nineties without knowledge of Stu Webb's collaborative divorce process and without contemplation of collaborative interdisciplinary practice. Their intention when choosing the term was that the role would be for mental health practitioners to coach clients through their divorce process.

So let's talk about the term "coach." Generally speaking, it has lost respect. Many, if not most, coaches prefer *not* to be called so. Why is that?

The word "coach" has a universal meaning that is not always respected because it is frequently abused . . . by "health coaches," "life coaches," "juice coaches," and all the other "coaches" out there who have no credentials. I know far too many consultants with no education or experience who call themselves "coaches" of one kind or another. "Life Coach," "Health Coach," "Divorce Coach," and "Business Coach" all leap to mind; I can name individuals who have co-opted that term with no credibility whatsoever. Thus, many consultants who have the credentials these days are avoiding the term entirely. It has become controversial in other industries, as well.

In contrast, the IACP requires a collaborative coach to have the following credentials:

1) A professional license in good standing in certain specific areas of mental health;
2) A minimum of 12 hours of introductory interdisciplinary collaborative training;
3) At least one 30-hour training in client-centered, facilitative conflict resolution;

4) Fifteen hours of training in professional coaching, communication skills, or advanced collaborative or mediation training; and

5) A minimum of three hours aimed at a basic understanding of family law.

Regardless, "coach" is the term upon which Thompson and Ross settled, that IACP has approved, and that has been in use in many communities now for 20 years. It also seems to be the term that the majority of collaborative communities use. Advocates for the term "coach" believe that changing the name now would cause even more confusion, creating yet another term to be used by some, but not all, communities. They worry about the practicality of changing the name because it would mean that all IACP references to "coach" on websites, marketing materials, etc. would need to be changed.

They also believe that we should respect the founders' terminology and their rationale for the term. According to Ross:

> Peggy and I chose the word "coach" with a great deal of thought and much debate in the collaborative community. While I agree anyone can call themselves a coach (or a facilitator or mediator for that matter), our practice groups' (and IACP's) requirement that a state license is necessary in order to be able to call oneself a "Collaborative Practice Divorce Coach" is insurance that we won't be mistaken for the general coach community. In the 25 years this has been in place in California, I know of no confusion. I think we as professionals are far more concerned than our clients, who seem to understand the requirements . . . . My mind does boggle at going back and changing all the literature and IACP requirements if we change the designation at this point.

So perhaps "collaborative coach" or "collaborative divorce

coach" or "CD coach" is the right answer here. "Coach" is certainly simple and straightforward. In which case, we need to get our outliers on track with everybody else.

I understand our mental health professionals' desire for distinct, creative titling. But none of the terms that we use to define this role throughout the English-speaking world seems quite right. Consider:

- COACH/COLLABORATIVE DIVORCE COACH/CDC: Although these terms define one of the roles of the mental health professional on the collaborative team, they do not consider the other hats that this professional wears. Often, especially in the one-coach model, the mental health professional leads the entire team, not just one or two of the spouses. Coaching is only one responsibility of the collaborative mental health practitioner. The term "coach" is simply not holistic or dynamic enough.

Further, as discussed above, people have lost respect for those labeled as "coach" as the word is too commonplace and often refers to folks with few credentials.

- ALIGNED COACH: In the two-coach model, each client has his own coach who is aligned with him. However, this term is not always appropriate because many communities utilize a one-coach model in which the coach is neutral.

- NEUTRAL: In the one-coach model, the coach is neutral. However, there are other neutral professionals in the collaborative process, like the financial professional and the child specialist. And in the two-coach model, the coach is not neutral. Thus, this is not a good word to describe this role.

- MENTAL HEALTH PROFESSIONAL: This is an accurate description, but when laypeople hear "mental health," they are immediately turned off. Most of them don't have mental health issues, so they feel they don't need this professional on their team. They may be offended you even suggested it. They may have never attended a therapy session or may have previously refused marital counseling. Although the mental health professional is not wearing his therapeutic hat in the collaborative setting, the layperson may not initially understand this and may refuse to proceed with the collaborative process simply because this term was used.

- MHP: This term is accurate regardless of what role the

professional is playing in a given case. The problem is that it is not user-friendly. And when people discover what it stands for, they really don't like it.

Moreover, the public does not like acronyms (or initialisms, which is actually what it is because it is pronounced letter-by-letter). Acronyms are helpful when used as an internal shorthand communication amongst colleagues, but when used with laypeople who are not clued in to the inner workings of a process, it comes across as intimidating jargon that can be both confusing and alienating. Using terminology that laypeople don't understand may cause them to question whether they really belong in the collaborative setting.

In this case, when an acronym has been created purely for the use of a specific group (collaborative professionals), it is often self-defeating. According to Bryan Garner, editor-in-chief of all current editions of *Black's Law Dictionary*:

> Although abbreviations are highly convenient, it's a false sense of convenience: they benefit the writer but burden the reader—unless they're already extremely well known, and most aren't.

> This burdening of the reader skews the reader-writer relationship. The whole idea instead is to make the reader's job easier, even if this means making the writer's job more difficult.

Instead of using acronyms, Garner suggests using succinct, real words.

- FACILITATOR: It is a hard word for some people to latch onto. Also, it is used by some communities to refer to the MHP and by other communities in the two-coach model to refer to the financial professional.
- FAMILY SPECIALIST: The coach does typically specialize in family conflict issues and act as the voice for the family, but this is just one responsibility of the coach.
- CHILD SPECIALIST: The role of the child specialist is distinguished from the role of the professional who we are trying to

define, who leads the collaborative team. The child specialist advocates for the voice of the child. The spouses may not even have children, so this term is not appropriate.

So, what title is the right title? When is jazzing up your job title taking it too far and how do you solve that problem?

> Answer: When your colorful language clutters comprehension.
> Solution: Write for the guy on the elevator.

As an undergrad at Yale, I studied English literature with a focus on creative writing. Later, after I got my law degree, after the inescapable hours of slaving over a hot computer, I zeroed in on my hobby, writing poetry. So, when I taught at Stetson University College of Law, in addition to the serious courses, I taught *Poetry Writing for Law Students and Their Professors*. I spent many hours sitting at a heavy wooden conference room table with aspiring lawyers (and their law professors) figuring out how best to communicate thoughts and feelings in print and, perhaps more importantly, how to communicate convincingly.

One of my law students once reiterated my mantra back to me: When you write, write for your avatar, the "guy on the elevator. He's not stupid; he's just tired."

Our avatar, too, is the guy on the elevator. He's tall; he's short. He's black; he's white; he's rich; he's poor. He's well-educated; he has a high school degree. He's anybody; he's everybody. He's:

- Excited,
- Confident,
- Concerned,
- Capable,
- Creative,
- Optimistic,
- Depressed,
- Doubtful, or
- Determined
- And any number of other possibilities.

The guy on the elevator—i.e. your intended client—needs to

know your exact role. The collaborative coach is someone who helps the clients to understand what their goals and interests really are, who helps to guide them to a resolution that meets their most important goals and interests, and who has many other responsibilities, depending on whether the team is using a one or two-coach model and whether he is working as the child specialist or as something else.

The collaborative process can be intimidating and perplexing to a client until he is actually cradled in it. Therefore, it is important to establish clarity in each professional's role to eliminate as much confusion as possible.

IACP has chosen a term. We respect the people involved in making that choice. But what if that decision hasn't kept pace with what has happened since? Certainly, the people who made that decision didn't have the benefit of the hindsight we do today. If they did, mightn't they admit that it's time to re-examine the issue?

Marketing is all about speaking the same language that the purchaser speaks. Good marketing involves clear branding so that the client has as clear expectations as possible, which helps to manage the collaborative process and outcome. The terms we are currently using are simply *not* universally understood or utilized, at least not yet. Let's change that.

We must either agree on the universal use of an already partially established term or choose a new term that is to be universally accepted. Can we identify a new term that is marketable and catchy and that more accurately describes the role of the mental health professional in the collaborative process?

In chemistry, a *catalyst* is any element or compound that initiates a reaction without fusing into it. A catalyst precipitates an event, in this case, the fair resolution to the end of the clients' marriage. The catalyst enables a reaction to proceed at an accelerated pace or under different conditions than otherwise possible. She provokes or speeds significant change or action. In CP, the MHP, like a catalyst, causes productive activity between two spouses by enabling them to openly discuss their goals and interests, thereby promoting fairer settlements than in litigation.

A catalyst is also someone whose talk, enthusiasm, or energy causes others to be more friendly, enthusiastic, or energetic. These are some of the behaviors that the collaborative catalyst models for the clients because these positive behaviors lead to the creation of better agreements.

Moreover, a catalyst is a person who causes change, and what greater change is there than the change that comes with divorce? The catalyst is the person who initiates and facilitates communication and then fades away into the background. A catalyst helps to restructure the family, and then, once the restructure is in place, steps aside and lets the family go. The catalyst does not take control; a catalyst cedes control to the divorcing couple and helps them learn the techniques to exercise that control, to take that leadership.

As the chapters of this anthology make plain, a collaborative divorce coach is a catalyst; she makes change happen for the divorcing couple. Consider whether we should adopt this term universally to describe the role of the mental health professional in the collaborative process.

---

[1] Ron Ousky, *Giving Collaborative Practice Permission to Grow.* IACP's Past President's Edition of the Collaborative Review (Volume 14, Issue 2, Fall 2014).

*Divorce professionals (whether mental health, legal, or financial) often burn out early due to the stress associated with dealing with individuals who are mourning the deaths of their once most treasured relationships. The unfairness and unpredictability of a courtroom divorce intensify the negativity, and what often pushes professionals to their limits is the feeling that they are not actually helping the individual or the family. For decades, people have been saying that there must be a better way.*

*And now there is. Collaborative practice offers a family an opportunity to work together with a team of professionals to craft a settlement agreement that meets the most important goals and interests of each of the spouses, as well as allows the children to safely have a voice in the matter when a child specialist is involved.*

*Collaborative professionals find their paths to collaborative practice in many different ways. Many experience a watershed moment when they know that they just can't continue in traditional divorce litigation. It may be watching a client unfairly receive a horrific, unexpected outcome in court. Or seeing children suffer due to protracted, expensive, unnecessary litigation. It may be based on the professional's own personal experience. It may even be as simple as receiving an invitation to a collaborative training at the right time, as in the following chapter. Whatever the reason, once a professional attends that first training, it is hard to deny the benefits of the process, not only on the clients, but also on the quality of life for the professional.*

## BEING OPEN
### BY LINDA SOLOMON, LPC, LMFT, LCDC

A number of years ago, Gwyneth Paltrow starred in a movie called "Sliding Doors." The movie begins with Gwyneth's character running down the stairs in the subway station to catch the next train. The door is closing as she arrives, and she manages to squeeze into a space on the train before it leaves. Her life then unfolds. In the middle of the movie, the above-described race down the stairs occurs again. This time, though, she does not make the train. We again proceed to watch her life unfold. Since watching that movie, I often use the term "sliding-door moments" to think about large or small events and choices that have changed the direction of my life. Working in collaborative practice as a neutral mental health professional (MHP) are clearly due to two, if not many, sliding-door moments that occurred for me.

Fourteen years ago, I was experiencing some symptoms of burnout when entering year 16 as a marriage and family therapist. I recognized the symptoms as I had experienced it to some degree at least twice before. For instance, ideas such as "you just need to go work in a bookstore or pack groceries for a while" were often entering my thoughts. At the same time, I received an invitation to attend a training on how to work in collaborative practice. Thinking I would not attend due to the cost and my already busy schedule, I left it on my kitchen island intending to recycle the flyer. One of my family members looked at the flyer and asked about the training. After hearing my concern about the registration fees, he simply said, "Well, all it will take is one client referral to make up the cost of the registration." Sliding Door Moment Number One! I signed up the next morning.

Texas, at the time, was working with a lawyer-only model. A group of professionals from around the state attended a two-day training. The trainers led us through two days of exercises to understand what was then called "The Collaborative Divorce Model." We learned about each client having a coach, the role of the coach, and the role of the child specialist. We also learned about the financial professional (FP) working as a neutral for the family and the process. It was a very interesting and challenging two days.

We were asked to sit with participants from the other disciplines and spent lots of time in role plays and small group discussion with our table members during the training. I was ready for the challenge and chose a table where I knew no one other than by name or face. What I didn't know at the time was I was seated next to a lawyer from Dallas who was held in the highest of regard by his peers. He had successfully litigated complex matters for many years and was deeply interested in working in the collaborative process. He had, at that time, worked on a few lawyer-only collaborative matters.

The morning after the training, I received a call from that lawyer asking me to lunch. He told me something I haven't forgotten because it made me giggle a bit and was also so humble and honest. He said, "I think I am pretty good at being a lawyer. What you know how to do, that I don't, is to talk to people in difficult situations. I like the words you use." He then pulled out a very small laminated piece of paper and told me that this was what he was using when things became difficult in meetings.

It said two things:

1. Tell me more about that.
2. When you ___, it makes you/I feel _____.

(I still like to tease him about that to this day.)

He then proceeded to tell me he was starting a new case and needed someone like me to be in the meetings to help with difficult discussions. He explained his thoughts as to why he preferred to work with one coach rather than two. (I later learned this was true for all of the lawyers who had attended that particular training.) He asked if I wanted to work on the case. Sliding Door Moment Number Two! Aaah, here is the one client I hoped to get to balance that registration fee. Of course, I said yes. I didn't know what I didn't know, to say the least. What I did know, however, was that I was trained in family systems and I knew how to handle group dynamics. I trusted myself, based on years of private practice, to figure out what needed to be said.

At the time, I was very grateful that I received such useful information about collaborative practice and the role of coaches in the two-coach model. It was helpful in terms of having a global understanding of our involvement in the process. I knew, though, that we needed to "make up" the role of the neutral as early cases evolved. I also knew that the lawyers and FPs were not the ones who could completely understand what neutral MHPs could offer and our ethical guidelines and boundaries. Luckily, there was another MHP with whom I frequently met who also received the training and was committed to working on this new role.

It was exciting and very challenging to create a role that had not been utilized to date. It quickly grew and became accepted as the norm in Texas. No one could have predicted that growth. There are a handful of lawyers in Austin, Ft. Worth, Houston, San Antonio, and Dallas who are the pioneers of this role. Each and every one of them (you know who you are) were willing to step out of their comfort zone (lawyer-only model), let go of some control, trust the neutrals to work with their clients, and be a member of a team. Add to all the above qualities a willingness on the part of all three disciplines to donate hundreds of unpaid hours on committees, writing forms, creating protocols for each discipline, and meeting regularly to evaluate each nuance of the role to decide if it worked or if something else was needed instead.

Others in this book will, I am sure, write about this model in detail. I will, for the purpose of this chapter, summarize it to say that the neutral facilitator's focus is on two systems: 1) the family system and 2) the team system. Both, as we all know, can be complex and demand much attention. When I began this work, I put most of my focus on the family system, somehow assuming the team system would work itself out. I quickly was reminded that any time a group of people comes together, the dynamics have to be worked through in a respectful way. In recent years, I have spent much of my time as a trainer asking professionals to take a closer look at the way they interact with others on the team and the positive or negative impact on the process and the clients.

During the first two to three years that we worked on developing this model and creating best practices, I was surprised how often I heard from the naysayers in various parts of North America. I was once pulled aside at a conference and asked, "When are you going to learn to do this work the right way?" I was told by a lawyer attendee at a training that this model had too many flaws and would "never help families." I was told that Texas was "causing problems" by creating another model and asked why we just couldn't do what everyone else was doing.

In one city, I was told that their lawyers are very strong

communicators, therefore, they wouldn't need neutral MHPs to help with communication. I knew, in that instance, that my response would make a difference in perception. I specifically remember that I responded, "It's not about lawyers being strong communicators. That is great. I am surrounded by lawyers in Dallas who are very skilled. It is about having neutrality in the process to balance advocacy." Those are just a few of the many interactions I remember.

My answer then, and my answer now, is the same. I believe that any model is valuable that is well thought out, based on family systems theory and group dynamics, and enriches this process. I don't think, nor have I ever thought, that there is only one way to do this work. I keep my focus on how to be a compassionate, effective neutral MHP.

In the collaborative process, we always ask clients not to become positional and to instead focus on interests. We ask them to brainstorm and to be open to considering an option they have never looked at before. By creating a new model in the early 2000s, weren't we asking the same of ourselves as professionals? Stay open. Don't become positional. Don't figuratively fold your arms and say, "No, that will never work." Instead, be open to hearing new ideas and possibilities.

As we move forward, I am reminded of a talk Stu Webb gave at an IACP Forum many years ago. I can see him standing at the podium looking through a kaleidoscope. I don't remember all the specific words, but I do remember the message, "Stay open to new models and new approaches. Keep pushing yourselves to do this difficult work in a better way. Stay focused. Stay creative." I am very excited to learn about the new approaches that I assume will grow over the next decade or so. I can't wait to learn some new skills that will help families during this difficult transition in their lives.

In the meantime, I want to give honor, respect, and a huge *thank you* to the hundreds of MHPs around the world who are so committed to using their expertise to help families, many of whom I have been privileged to mentor, train, and learn from every day. The clients and other professionals are so lucky to have you!

Linda Solomon, LPC, LMFT, LCDC, is a licensed professional counselor, licensed chemical dependency counselor, and licensed marriage and family therapist. She has been in private practice in Dallas, Texas, for 30 years. Her work with individuals, couples, and families has focused on relationship issues and addictive behaviors. She is actively involved in the collaborative team approach as a neutral mental health professional and was instrumental in the development of the role. She is also trained as a mediator and a parenting coordinator.

Ms. Solomon has presented training on coaching and collaborative practice nationally in locations such as New York, Boston, Florida, Minneapolis, Colorado, and Pittsburgh and internationally in Ireland, Australia, Canada, and New Zealand. She has presented at numerous IACP forums on such diverse topics as the role of the neutral mental health professional, balancing neutrality in the process, and a comparison of the one coach and two coach team approaches. Ms. Solomon is also a member of the IACP trainers committee.

Ms. Solomon is a member of the Lone Star Collaborative Training team and serves as a mentor to other mental health professionals in various parts of the world. She is a former board member of IACP and the Collaborative Law Institute of Texas. Ms. Solomon served as chairperson of the CLI-TX collaborative conference in 2011. She is very proud to be the 2015 recipient of The Gay Cox Collaborative Spirit Award in the State of Texas.

Ms. Solomon continues to be committed to helping collaborative practice spread throughout the world, with a particular focus on the team approach. She is passionate about her profession having a clear understanding of the role on a collaborative team and helping the other professions understand how mental health professionals contribute to the process.

*One of the many challenges that a collaborative professional experiences is to convince his client that including a mental health professional on the collaborative team is not only beneficial but will ultimately save him time and money. Many clients will not initially see the value in the MHP and will want to save money by not including one on the team. Additionally, a client may be somewhat offended at the suggestion, perhaps believing that he doesn't need therapy. But although a mental health professional is trained as a therapist, he wears a different hat when he works on a collaborative team.*

*It is important for the professional to explain to the client that the collaborative MHP does not act as a therapist. Rather, his role is to guide the team through the process and to ensure that the team stays focused and productive. Because of the MHP's education and experience, he is better able to read the clients and the professionals and to redirect the team when emotional or psychological roadblocks arise. The MHP better understands the unique personalities of the individuals involved, as well as the underlying factors that could lead to impasse.*

*By including an MHP on the collaborative team, a client stands a far better chance of resolving his matter quickly and effectively. In a vast majority of resolved collaborative cases, clients report that the MHP was a vital member of the collaborative team.*

## EMOTIONAL CONTROL IN THE COLLABORATIVE PROCESS
### BY BRUCE R. FREDENBURG, M.S., LMFT

A man sat across from me in my office. He was a tidy looking man, wearing a freshly pressed collared shirt with a striped tie and navy pleated dress pants. He had a short, professional haircut and no facial hair. He had impeccable posture. I had barely introduced myself when he said:

My divorce attorney wants me to get a divorce coach. Why would I want a divorce coach? I'm a practical, bottom-line kind of person. I look at a problem and gather what I need. I understand I need a lawyer, and I can understand why a financial person could be helpful, but why a divorce coach?

He added, "I have a therapist, and she is helping me. We already tried a marriage counselor, and that didn't work."

Having been asked this question time and time again, I knew just how to respond:

That is a good question. Divorce has two tracks, and they operate simultaneously. There is the business track and the emotional track. Even in non-adversarial processes like collaborative divorce and mediation, the emotional track, if not handled well, can easily knock the business track off course and create enormous damage to your family, including your children, as well as cost you much more money and time.

"Well I certainly don't want that," he replied. "I am very stressed, and I can already see how it is all impacting on our children. But I just don't see why I need yet another professional involved in this process."

"I understand where you are coming from." I continued:

A licensed therapist trained specifically to work with divorcing couples can minimize this danger by serving as a divorce coach or as a neutral child specialist. A divorce coach's role is to assist you through the difficult emotions that can create impasse and impede the collaborative and mediation efforts. The right divorce coach combines years of experience and skills in conflict resolution to create a synergy to balance the legal and emotional aspects of divorce.

In addition, in a collaborative divorce or in a mediated divorce process, a divorce coach will help you find the expertise of other collaborative and mediation trained experts, such as a neutral financial professional who is certified in the financial complexities of divorce or a neutral child specialist who has expertise and experience working with children and parents going through divorce.

"I suppose I can see how a divorce coach might be helpful. Tell me more about a child specialist's role. I'm really concerned about the effect the divorce is having on our children."

I explained:

A licensed therapist who has the right additional training and experience can help your family by serving as a neutral child specialist, or an NCS. An NCS will meet with you, your spouse, and your children, both individually and jointly, and bring the voices of your children into the collaborative or mediation process. This keeps your children in the center of your divorce, not the middle. You and your spouse can also agree to consult with the NCS post-settlement as the needs of you and your children change and evolve.

"Well, divorce coaches and child specialists do seem to have important roles," he mused. "But I'm just not convinced that it is worth the money."

I realized he needed just a bit more of an explanation. "Let me tell you a little story that might help you appreciate the importance of these professionals." I began:

A teacher walked around a room while teaching

stress management to an audience. As she raised a glass of water, everyone expected they'd be asked the "half empty or half full" question. Instead, with a smile on her face, she inquired, "How heavy is this glass of water?"

Answers ranged from 8 oz. to 20 oz.

She replied, "The absolute weight doesn't matter. It depends on how long I hold it. If I hold it for a minute, it's not a problem. If I hold it for an hour, I'll have an ache in my arm. If I hold it for a day, my arm will feel numb and paralyzed. In each case, the weight of the glass doesn't change, but the longer I hold it, the heavier it becomes.

The stresses and worries in life are like that glass of water. Think about them for a while and nothing happens. Think about them a bit longer, and they begin to hurt. And if you think about them all day long, you will feel paralyzed—incapable of doing anything. Remember to put the glass down.

Wrapping up, I concluded, "This story has been told in various versions. Although I do not know the source of this tale, the point of the story here is that, as a divorce coach, I teach people how to put the glass down."

That did the trick. "Okay, I'm convinced. Where do I sign?"

## HOW DOES A DIVORCE COACH TEACH PEOPLE HOW TO "PUT THE GLASS DOWN"?

Divorce is rated as one of the most stressful life experiences a person will ever have. When overcome by anger, fear, or sadness, many people turn to their attorney for guidance and help. The problem with that is that, while attorneys are well trained in the law, they do not have the training to deal with these problems with the same level of expertise as a licensed therapist. So even when they do the best they can, it is no more effective than it would be to ask a mental health professional to solve one's legal or financial problems. The therapist may have acquired knowledge about those issues, but it is not the same as asking an attorney about law or a financial specialist about financial concerns.

When a couple has reached the point that one or both of them decide to divorce, communication has usually deteriorated. Over time, every argument is connected to every other disagreement. A vicious cycle develops. It is hard or impossible to have any important discussions. The most frequent emotions they experience when they try to talk are anger, fear, and sadness. These emotions create biochemical changes in our bodies and brains, which make rational, honest communication very difficult. A licensed therapist trained as a divorce coach has the knowledge to help clients minimize and even eliminate many of those problems. The divorce coach can teach divorcing couples new skills to help them communicate and effectively plan for their post-divorce futures.

## THE FIGHT, FLIGHT, OR FREEZE RESPONSE

Imagine that, fifty thousand years ago, one of your ancestors knelt down by a river to get a drink of water. Just when she knelt, a "log" floating near the shore turned out to be a crocodile and tried to attack her. To survive, she had to react instantly by recognizing the threat, and, within a tiny fraction of a second, jumping back at full speed and running away or fighting it off. We know you are descended from someone who had that ability because the others were killed or eaten.

As soon as your ancestor perceived a threat, her brain sent messages to her body to release hormones, such as adrenaline and cortisol, that trigger a whole cascade of reactions. The heart races. Blood pressure increases to move blood away from your hands and feet (that's why mood rings work; they detect cold fingers when you are stressed) and into the major muscle groups and the brain so you can effectively fight or flee. It even moves blood away from your digestive system, which interferes with other aspects of your health. But in a life or death situation, who cares? Eventually, the

11

physical activities of fighting, fleeing, or freezing turn off the system.

These responses happen in our brain and our body whenever we worry, think about problems, or are aroused by pain or anxiety. It is part of our evolutionary history and actually helped early humans survive. It can also interfere with sleep.

Here's the catch. At the same time that all of that "alarm" activity is going on, chemical signals are sent to switching stations in other parts of the brain to remember everything that happens in great detail. That's so you will recognize the danger sooner next time.

Some months or years later, here is your ancestor once again walking through the forest, when out of the corner of her eye, she sees a real log. She might not take any conscious notice, but the automatic parts of the brain remember that "logs" can be crocodiles, so the brain and body react biochemically exactly the same way they would if it was a crocodile.

These hormones were especially important in helping our ancient ancestors meet the challenges of more primitive times when human beings were hunters facing regular danger from wild beasts and predators. A life or death situation may trigger this response, but the brain may respond in a similar fashion to persistent lower levels of stress. Nowadays, we don't see many crocodiles or bears, so emotional stresses have replaced physical ones. Pain can also trigger this response.

As a result, we can't usually take the physical actions necessary to dissipate the stimulation of these hormones. So these powerful substances tend to "attack" the body instead of enabling it to deal better with outside forces. If a stress response is chronic, the constant presence of stress hormones begins to wear down the body's immunological system; whatever part of the body is weakest will show signs of dysfunction first.

And, of course, it interferes with sleeping, which creates additional problems.

Our brains have a negative bias. They pay more attention to negative events or thoughts than they do to positive events. Our brains are concerned with pattern recognition and are constantly scanning for possible threats. This was part of how our early ancestors survived, by anticipating threats (both real and imagined) ahead of time.

There is a well-known study that demonstrates this negative prejudice. Using a functional magnetic resonance image (FMRI) machine, researchers flashed the word "no" in front of someone for a fifth of a second (too fast to consciously see). The reaction, they discovered, was that a part of the brain activates the body's fight, flight, or freeze response. That's why, eventually, all negative encounters and arguments become linked so that just the thought of your spouse or a certain facial expression can trigger the fight, flight, or freeze. (By the way, nothing much happens when you flash the word "yes.")

On top of that, your spouse is having the same experiences.

It is obvious that none of those three (fight, flight, or freeze) responses improves communication. A divorce coach who has the right training and experience can help you remove yourself from those emotional states so you can dampen down your conflicts and move forward in ways that are much better for your family.

In addition to whatever is going on between you and your spouse, your attorney and financial specialist are also human beings whose brains operate the same way. That means a facial expression, tone of voice, or something else not related to the current situation can also (in only a fifth of a second) trigger her fight, flight, or freeze response. This usually creates a fleeting look on her face that can subconsciously trigger others in the meetings and result in poorer outcomes. An experienced licensed therapist trained to work with divorce teams is alert to this and will act to interrupt it before significant problems erupt.

Here are just a few of the ways a licensed mental health professional taking on this role adds value:

- A divorce coach monitors the emotional climate of everyone present during the "business" meetings, including his own, and acts proactively to interdict escalations before they disrupt the process.
- Sometimes a topic is so painful for one spouse that he will say "yes" to a proposal when he actually means, "I can't bear to talk about this for one more minute." A divorce coach assists the clients and other professionals to understand when an apparent agreement is just an attempt to get a "time out" from a client who is

in so much distress he is masquerading agreement as a conflict avoidant pain control strategy.

- A divorce coach teaches clients how to take personal responsibility for their own emotional states and how to reduce and interrupt feelings of anger, anxiety, fear, and sadness that would keep them stuck and unable to make good, clear decisions.

I recently taught a group of family law attorneys, financial specialists, and therapists a specific meditative technique that shifts a person's emotional state from fear and anger to a more peaceful state in only a few minutes. It uses guided imagery and visualization to create mental and then physical changes in the body to minimize the negative effects of the hormones involved in anger and fear.

Two weeks later, a financial specialist colleague of mine reported being in one of those necessary business meetings required in divorce. One of the spouses was so hurt and angry over her sense of betrayal and loss that she was unable to participate in this meeting in which the couple was intending to make major, final agreements. The client alternated between yelling, crying, accusing, and withdrawing. All of these reactions were understandable, but they also prevented any agreements that would serve the family.

The divorce coach and the collaborative attorney called a "time out" and went into a private meeting with their client. They then helped her experience that meditative technique. They emerged 15 minutes later, and there was a complete and noticeable difference. The client was calm, cooperative, and mentally present. The couple then successfully co-created agreements that met the needs of the whole family.

My colleague could hardly believe it; now she refuses to meet with any clients going through divorce unless they agree to retain divorce coaches.

## HOW TO FIND A QUALIFIED, COMPETENT DIVORCE COACH

The rise of the use of the terms "divorce coach," "life coach," and the like has confused people who need qualified help. There are divorce coaches whose own marketing materials offer as their qualifications that, after suffering through their own divorce, they graduated from a life coaching program that offers a certification in divorce coaching. One program that "certifies" life coaches consists of less than 20 sessions totaling 52 hours, including practicum. Another offers a certification program entailing three days, including one day of marketing training. Not much in the way of true certification!

A 2012 Reuters article warns of the emergence of coaches with little education, experience, and certifications:

> Just as the 1990s brought the rise of life coaches, the new millennium is the age of the divorce coach. It's a concept that appears to have started with Dr. Kim Lurie, a Merrick, New York, attorney who began calling herself a divorce coach in the 1990s. The phrase "divorce coach" doesn't begin turning up in newspaper archives until the 2000s, when attorneys, financial mediators, psychotherapists and other professionals began reinventing themselves and calling themselves divorce coaches.
>
> In recent years, businesses around the country have taken divorce coaching to a new level: a couple works with several coaches, each specializing in things such as finances and co-parenting.
>
> The key to finding a competent divorce coach is researching your coach's background—whether it's law, finance or counseling—and deciding if it will lend itself to helping you navigate your divorce. Some divorce coaches do receive specialized training, but if you aren't careful, you could wind up hiring a divorce coach whose only experience is having been divorced. The industry is in its infancy even as its (mostly) affluent clients struggle with very grown-up problems.

## WHAT'S THE DIFFERENCE BETWEEN COACHING AND THERAPY?

Therapists are primarily concerned with helping people create more productive and joyful present and future lives. As divorce coaches, we have a specific focus. The focus is on change that will support our client's ability to sufficiently manage his own emotional states to be able to better participate in the necessary business-focused meetings of a divorce so that he is ready to enter into an agreement when required.

A licensed mental health professional acting in the role of a divorce coach takes specific training to be able to work effectively with other divorce professionals. The goal of the professionals is to help clients who are in the midst of an extraordinarily stressful life event have a more peaceful and respectful divorce process that takes into account the needs of the entire family. The divorce coach uses all of his therapeutic skills to help clients achieve this. There needs to be a more accurate distinction between coaching versus therapy. Someone who is not a therapist but calls herself a "divorce coach" cannot offer the same level of expertise and skill.

In the mid-1990s in Northern California, pioneers Peggy Thompson, Ph.D., and Nancy Ross, LCSW, began building interdisciplinary teams to better serve divorcing couples and their families. They conceptualized the role of the collaborative divorce coach (CDC), who is a licensed mental health professional who assists clients with communication skills, emotional regulation, stress management, identification of interests and goals, conflict resolution skills, co-parenting skills, and co-parenting plan development.

At www.collaborativepractice.com, you will find a list of licensed therapists who are also trained as divorce coaches and child specialists near you, as well as information on their qualifications.

Bruce Fredenburg, M.S., LMFT, with board certification in clinical hypnosis, has been a California-licensed marriage and family therapist since 1982, specializing in divorce-related issues and blended families. He has extensive training in mediation and in the fully integrated interdisciplinary team model of collaborative practice, and he has also trained in the one-coach model. He is trained and experienced in the management of chronic pain, dealing with trauma, chemical dependency, and addictions.

As one of the founding members of Collaborative Divorce Solutions of Orange County (CDSOC) in 2003, he serves as a divorce coach, child specialist, and case manager. Mr. Fredenburg has held the position of chair of CDSOC's training and education committee, which provides monthly training for the practice group. He is on the leadership team for the Collaborative Divorce Education Institute (CDEI), which is a non-profit organization whose mission is to provide excellent training for collaborative professionals, as well as education for the public about peaceful and respectful solutions for families who are restructuring before, during, and after the divorce process. As a member of CDEI's training team, he trains attorneys, mental health professionals, and financial specialists in various aspects of collaborative divorce.

Mr. Fredenburg has been a presenter multiple times at the International Academy of Collaborative Professionals' annual forum and at CP Cal, California's annual statewide conference for collaborative professionals. He has appeared on the Time Warner Public television series *How to Get a Divorce*. Mr. Fredenburg was recruited to create and teach parenting classes for adoptive and foster parents for County of Orange Social Services Agency. An award-winning speaker, he has presented training programs for corporations, government agencies, schools, and professional associations since 1989.

He has published articles on male-female communication for *Sharing Ideas*, a national magazine dedicated to professional speakers, trainers, and meeting planners. In 1996, he was awarded Speaker of the Year by the Professional Speakers Network. Mr. Fredenburg is the author of several audio learning and self-help programs, including *Men and Women: How to Understand Each Other, Take the Pain Out of Change,* and *Profound Relaxation.* Mr. Fredenburg's most recent self-help programs are *Sleep Solution* and *Anxiety Solution;* both are available on Amazon.

When children are involved, including a child specialist on the collaborative team gives the children a legitimate voice in the matter. While parents should shield children from the intricacies of divorce as much as possible, in certain situations, especially when older children are involved, it is important for them to feel as though they are being heard. Additionally, when parents suffer from addictions or mental health issues, or when domestic violence or power imbalances are involved, a professional whose sole purpose is to stand up for the rights of the children can be a crucial addition to the team.

The child specialist is also better equipped to prepare the parenting plan and such an expert usually bills at a lower hourly rate than any attorney who might draft the timesharing plan if a child specialist or other mental health professional was not included on the team.

The child specialist develops special relationships with the children at a time when they may be questioning their closest bonds. She also coaches the parents on issues like how to discuss the divorce with their children, how to address behavioral issues that may arise due to the divorce, and how to better co-parent and communicate after the divorce. She ensures that the children's needs are met during the divorce and that the parenting plan assures that they will continue to be met after the divorce.

## THE CHILD SPECIALIST
### BY CAROL R. HUGHES, PH.D., LMFT

"Divorce is a different experience for children and adults because the children lose something that is fundamental to their development—the family structure. The family comprises the scaffolding upon which children mount successive developmental stages, from infancy into adolescence."[1]

Every year in the United States, over one million children experience the pain of their parents' divorce.[2] World-renowned child therapist Haim Ginnott asserted, "Children are like wet cement. Whatever falls on them leaves an impression." Divorce is a traumatic and deeply painful transition for both adults and children, and it affects the entire family. The loss of the intact family unit is destabilizing for children, for their parents, and for their family and community support systems. Minor and adult children frequently report that their parents' divorce was the most profound loss they have ever experienced.

Research tells us that divorce is the second highest stressor for human beings, second only to the death of a loved one. For both minor and adult children, their parents' divorce is like a death in that they experience the demise of their intact family. When a couple decides to separate and/or divorce, especially when they have children, the familial and community relationships do not disappear. They continue. But in what form do they continue? Hostile, neutral, cooperative?

Many families will enter into a legal process that will, in many if not most cases, be extremely damaging to these relationships. When couples litigate, what we call "combat divorce," they enter an adversarial process designed to escalate conflict, not de-escalate it. Conflict damages relationships rather than heals them. Often litigating attorneys tell their clients, "Do not talk with your spouse. Talk to me. I will talk with your spouse's attorney." How can such couples then be expected to work together to create an effective co-parenting plan that minimizes the conflict that is so damaging to their children? Research states that the number one predictor of children's adjustment during and post-divorce is the level of conflict between their parents.

Divorce researcher Judith Wallerstein states that children are the "hidden clients" in divorce and that they have not been given an opportunity to express their concerns or feelings regarding the dissolution of their family.

In 1989, the United Nations Convention on the Rights of Children established that in all matters affecting the child, the views of the child will be "given due weight in accordance with the age and maturity of the child." In Australia, child-inclusive mediation evolved as an enactment of these United Nations principles, enabling children to present their wishes in family law proceedings about them. In child-inclusive mediation, the child specialist (CS) actually speaks with the children and subsequently consults with parents and the mediator. Research regarding child-inclusive mediation reveals that there are more positive outcomes, including improved emotional availability of both parents to their children and more parent and child contentment with the parenting plan.

Sadly, in 2010 the California Elkins Family Law Implementation Task Force found that 80% of child custody mediators do not include children in the process, resulting in children having parenting plans imposed on them without their input.

Family lawyer and adjunct law school professor Bart Carey tells his clients that until a couple decides to separate or divorce, they never consult law books about what to do with their goals, interests, and values. Further, judges cannot always do what is best for the family and the children because they only have a range of options that the court can exercise. He advises his clients, "Children should be heard and not seen. . . . The child specialist gives your child an independent voice in the room and provides you as parents the insights you might otherwise miss."

The non-adversarial, respectful divorce process offered in collaborative divorce provides parents the opportunity to learn how to improve their communication so they can decrease, not increase, their conflict and write a new story of mutual cooperation for their children's benefit.

## WHO IS THE CS?

The International Academy of Collaborative Professionals' minimum standards for the CS include licensure as a mental health professional; background, education, and experience in family systems; expertise in child development; clinical experience with a specialty focus on children and in-depth understanding of children's unique issues in divorce; twelve hours collaborative training; at least one thirty-hour training in client-centered facilitative conflict resolution; fifteen hours additional training in coaching, communication, or advanced mediation; and three hours basic understanding of family law in the CS's own jurisdiction. The CS may assist the family post-divorce in divorce-related matters for the children, however, the CS shall never engage in a dual role with clients. For example, the CS in a collaborative divorce or mediation process shall never become the children's therapist. Nor shall the CS have been the children's therapist prior to the collaborative divorce or mediation process.

## HOW DOES THE CS GATHER INFORMATION?

The CS may employ a combination of any of the below or any other information gathering tools deemed appropriate for the family:

- Meets the co-parents together and/or alone to hear each co-parent's hopes, goals, and concerns to gain an understanding of each co-parent's view of the children and to observe the co-parents' dynamics;
- If there are siblings, meets the children first in their sibling unit;
- Meets each child alone to determine his/her needs and wants;
- Meets each child together with each co-parent and may meet together with siblings;
- May meet the children and the co-parents in their home(s) or another out-of-office environment;
- Utilizes questionnaires and inventories completed by the children, co-parents, and collateral resources to gather information;
- May gather information, with appropriate signed releases, from collateral sources (teachers, therapists, child care providers, etc.). As a protection for the children, the integrity of the process, and the collateral sources, collateral communications are not shared with the rest of the professional team or the co-parents, unless with specific releases from collateral sources. The CS *never* divulges information about the case to the collateral sources. Information goes one way only—from the collateral contact to the CS;
- Continuously communicates with divorce coaches

throughout the process about co-parenting issues, family dynamics, and any and all pertinent information that assists the co-parents to effectively co-parent their children, become agreement ready, and co-create their agreements;

- Shares the information, as appropriate, with the divorce coaches in the five-way co-parent/divorce coaches/CS meeting; and/or

- Continuously gathers information from all interactions with children, co-parents, and all professional team members.

## WHAT DOES THE CS DO?

The CS:

- Provides a neutral, non-judgmental environment where children ask questions and share their perceptions and feelings about the changes occurring in their family;

- Elicits children's experience of co-parents' parenting skills;

- Focuses on "child's best interests" that may seem counter to "child's voice";

- Seeks to understand each co-parent's hopes, goals, and concerns for their children and their child(ren)'s futures;

- Highlights co-parents' common underlying interests;

- Assists co-parents to understand the post-separation/divorce needs of each child;

- Educates co-parents about how to enhance their children's adjustment to the divorce and co-parenting plan;

- Educates co-parents about factors which enhance or endanger children's adjustment to divorce;

- Elicits a shared vision from the co-parents regarding their respective involvement in each child's life in the present and future (which may include initial and future co-parenting plan ideas);

- Educates co-parents about their children's needs based on getting to know the children;

- Encourages co-parents to begin to co-author a new story of cooperation;

- Assists co-parents to understand each child's possible living preferences and concerns about present co-parenting;

- Provides co-parents with the information they need to

better understand what is happening to the children and to make important co-parenting decisions;

- Provides relevant information to the collaborative professional team;
- Educates about conflict disengagement and effective co-parenting;
- Gives difficult feedback to co-parents, when necessary; and/or
- Assists the co-parents and the other collaborative professional team members to craft a co-parenting plan for children and co-parents that meets the needs of each child and the co-parents.

Children will often tell a CS their real feelings when telling their parents only what they think their parents want to hear. When children have a neutral professional who only cares about their needs, listens to them, and speaks for them, they are often more accepting of a co-parenting plan.

## WHAT DOES THE CS CONSIDER?

- Developmental issues (e.g. the needs of a four-year-old, ten-year-old, or 22-year-old are quite different);
- Temperament of each child and each co-parent;
- Each child's relationship to family members;
- Extended family and community relationships;
- Particular strengths/resilience of each child;
- The child's current reaction(s) to the family changes: worries, fears, hopes, preferences; and/or
- Special vulnerabilities (e.g. learning difficulties, emotional distress, disabilities, substance abuse, etc.).

Children experience the same divorce differently from how their parents experience it. By definition, parents are unable to see the divorce from the perspective of their children.

The CS brings the voice of the children into the divorce process and serves on the professional team as a neutral representative of the children's needs and preferences in the divorce process and the restructuring family. During meetings, with photos of the children on the table, the physical presence of the CS holds the children's place at the table and helps co-parents be mindful that every decision they make will impact their children.

## How Do the Children Benefit?

Each child has:
- A safe place with a neutral professional to share his story about what's happening in the family;
- An opportunity to ask questions and get clarification about the changes in the family;
- Support and comfort during a stressful time and a sense that he has a voice in the process; and
- Relief by bringing to the co-parents' attention problems, worries, fears, and hopes that may have gone undetected or unexpressed.

## How Do the Co-Parents Benefit?

The co-parents have:
- New information and the opportunity to consider the special needs and concerns of each child;
- Information about their child's point of view;
- Help in understanding the specific worries and concerns of each child;
- Discussion regarding the anticipated challenges and difficulties inherent in co-parenting;
- Help in identifying and appreciating their common interests as co-parents; and
- Input regarding their co-parenting plan, whether the children are minors or adults, because all children, whether minors or adults, benefit from their co-parents working together for the children's benefit.

## A Frightened Boy

I met Sean, a shy ten-year-old boy suffering from anxiety, when I became the CS on his parents' collaborative divorce team. His parents had a history of engaging in volatile arguments in front of him and his older sister and had spent minimal time talking with him or his sister about their impending divorce process. Sean confided in me:

> I feel so alone and confused, especially now that Mom and Dad are getting a divorce. My sister is off with her friends, and even though Mom and Dad live in different houses now, they still argue and yell at each other every time they see each other. I wish I had no ears. When I am at Mom's, I am afraid I will never see Dad again, and when I am at Dad's, I'm afraid I will never see Mom again. I can't sleep because I worry so much. All I want is for them to stop fighting and be friends.

I thought about the research that appropriate information helps children cope with changes and reduces anxiety and that the typical parent spends only ten minutes explaining the divorce experience to his children, as well as the research that children exposed to high conflict have significantly poorer emotional and behavioral adjustment than those exposed to low conflict.

Virtually all parents want to do what is best for their children, but they often don't realize that what they are doing is actually harming their children. I listened as Sean shared his feelings, and I answered his questions. During our one-on-one meeting, I helped him be able to share his feelings and concerns with his mom and dad, and I subsequently educated his parents about the damage that their high conflict was causing him. Sean's parents were able to hear how important it was for them to create a co-parenting plan that met Sean's needs, de-escalated their conflict, and reassured Sean that he would not lose either of them.

A year after Sean's co-parents completed their collaborative divorce, Sean told them that he wanted to meet with me. As he sat down on the couch in my office, a big smile stretched across his face.

He told me,

> You won't believe what happened! The other day I

26

heard Mom talking on the phone. I wondered who she was talking to. I thought it was one of her good friends. She sounded so happy and friendly. Then I heard her say Dad's name! That's all I ever wanted—for them to stop fighting and just be friends. And, I'm able to sleep ok at both houses now. Thank you for helping me and my parents!

## WHAT ABOUT ADULT CHILDREN?

Brian Don Levy, collaborative lawyer, mediator, and trainer, shares with his clients who are contemplating choosing a collaborative divorce or team mediation divorce process:

Having a child specialist on a collaborative divorce team is an absolute necessity for me as a collaborative attorney, especially if the children are adult children. When I was a litigator, I used to tell my clients that after their children turn 18, they are no longer minor children, no longer subject to the court's jurisdiction, and no longer part of the equation. I now understand that adult children of a divorcing family do matter—all children of a divorcing family matter. Divorcing parents are redefining the legacy they leave to their children no matter what the age of the child. They model how adults solve problems, and their children learn from watching how their parents approach the divorce—it is either a "battle to be won" or a "problem to be solved." What is at stake is what children in restructuring families learn from their parents, and what they take with them into their relationships. Adult children can easily become the confidant of a parent, the hidden voice in the background trying to influence a parent, or an influencer trying to steer a parent towards safety or into a position of interest. With the increasing numbers of "grey divorces," I am also

27

seeing increasing numbers of divorces with adult
children. Having the child specialist on board from
the beginning equips the professional team and
the family to aid the parents in co-creating healthy
agreements, while allowing the children to be in
the center rather than in the middle.

Mary and John were the "all-American" couple. They were
college sweethearts and had been married for over 30 years. They
had two grown children, both of whom were married with children
of their own. Since our collaborative practice community most
frequently uses the full team model consisting of two collaborative
lawyers, two divorce coaches, one neutral financial professional,
and one neutral CS, the professionals shared with John and Mary
the value that the adult CS would bring to their collaborative
divorce process. Mary and John were enthusiastic about including
me as the adult CS on their collaborative divorce team.

Right before their first full team financial co-creating
agreements meeting, John called his divorce coach to tell him that
their son had been arrested the night before for driving under the
influence (DUI) and that this was not his first DUI. During the
professional team pre-meeting held immediately prior to John and
Mary joining the professionals for the meeting, John's divorce coach
shared John's concern and that John had discussed it with Mary. The
professional team thought that Mary and John would have a very
difficult time concentrating on the business of the financial co-
creating agreements meeting if they did not address their concerns
about their son. The professional team decided to offer the couple
the opportunity to speak in a three-way meeting with me prior to
the meeting beginning.

During the three-way meeting, I listened to John's and Mary's
concerns, briefly educated them about alcohol abuse, and offered to
provide them with appropriate referrals.

It was immediately apparent that their anxiety level dropped
significantly. After the three-way meeting, reassured that they had
a plan to assist their son, they were able to move into the financial
meeting and successfully co-create their financial agreements.

## WHAT DO PARENTS SAY ABOUT HAVING A NEUTRAL CS FOR THEIR COLLABORATIVE DIVORCE PROCESS?

Steve, a father of three minor children says:

> It was especially helpful in our collaborative team meeting that the CS sat across from us at the meetings with picture collages of our children depicting things that she learned in talking with them that were important to them. As we looked from papers to people across the table these were great visuals of our children as reminders that we will always be a family, a restructured family, that our children had concerns about themselves and about our welfare, and that financial decisions we were making would affect them if we were not wise in our decision making and planning.

Jennifer, the mother of a teenager and a young adult child shares:

> One of the main focuses of our divorce was that our children were part of it. They loved the fact that they had a say in it and that they were not pushed aside. What was most dynamic was that during the actual collaborative meetings, there were pictures of our children on the table in front of the CS to remind us that there was someone there representing them and that they were there in the meetings with us. It helped us focus back to them as a family as a whole rather than to us as individuals, meeting just our needs. They were able to express their concerns and what was going to happen to them. It helped bring our children back together. It helped them develop a relationship with each of us, as their parents, so that we can now easily be in the same setting with them without any problems or discussions about

divorce, or anything else, and have a normal life again. We have better relationships now, six years down the road.

Imagine creating more peace in the world one child, one family at a time!

---

[1] Wallerstein, F., & Blakeslee, S., *Second Chances: Men, Women and Children a Decade After Divorce* (New York: Mariner Books, 2004)

[2] Emery, R. E., *The Truth About Children and Divorce: Dealing with the Emotions So You and Your Children Can Thrive* (New York: Penguin Group, 2004)

Carol R. Hughes, Ph.D., LMFT, is a California licensed psychotherapist who has been in private practice since 1983. She holds her doctorate degree in clinical psychology and her master's degree in counseling psychology, achieving both *summa cum laude* and *Phi Beta Kappa* honors. She is also a two-time Fulbright Scholar. Dr. Hughes holds her board certification in hypnotherapy, is a Level II EMDR therapist, and served as an associate professor of human services at Saddleback College for ten years.

At the tender age of four years old, Dr. Hughes experienced her parents' high conflict divorce, which gave her firsthand experience of the pain such divorces can cause children, their parents, and their extended families and communities. During her many years in private practice providing services for families experiencing the adversarial divorce process, she kept searching for more peaceful, respectful divorce processes. This led her to becoming trained in collaborative divorce and mediation.

In 2003, she became one of the founding members of Collaborative Divorce Solutions of Orange County (CDSOC). She provides services as a divorce coach, child specialist, and team/case manager and serves on the board of directors. Dr. Hughes has extensive training in mediation and in the interdisciplinary team model of collaborative practice. She frequently trains and mentors collaborative practitioners. She has appeared on the Time Warner Public television series *How to Get a Divorce*, has written numerous articles about divorce and its effects on children and families, and her interviews have been featured in publications such as the *New York Times* and *Bottom Line Personal*.

Dr. Hughes is a frequent presenter at the annual conferences of the International Academy of Collaborative Professionals, Collaborative Practice California (CP Cal), and the California chapter of the Association of Family Conciliation Courts. Dr. Hughes is also a co-founder of the Collaborative Divorce Education

Institute, whose mission is to educate the public about peaceful options for divorce and to provide quality training for collaborative divorce professionals. In April 2011, CP Cal honored Dr. Hughes with the Eureka Award, which recognizes those who have made significant contributions and demonstrated an abiding dedication to establishing and sustaining collaborative practice in California.

For a complete listing of her collaborative practice training and teaching workshops, visit www.CollaborativePractice.com, the website of the International Academy of Collaborative Professionals, and click on the "Locate a Collaborative Professional near you" link. In addition, please visit Dr. Hughes' website www.DivorcePeacemaking.com.

Perhaps the most important ancillary service in Dr. Hughes' practice is Amahle (Molly), a loving yellow Labrador. She is Dr. Hughes' canine co-therapist, i.e., therapy dog, and she is a very good listener.

Dr. Hughes lives in southern California with her husband, Nick. Her favorite pastimes are running with Molly on the beach while Nick surfs, tending to her garden, and vacationing with their adult children.

*One of the most difficult moments in a divorce is telling your child that his biggest fear is becoming reality. The way that you share with your child that you are getting divorced will set the tone for how he handles the divorce. Even when a child expects the news, it is still shattering for him to finally hear the truth, especially when both parents are highly involved in the child's life. Learning that he will have to split time between his parents and live in two separate houses can be devastating and scary.*

*A parent must treat this moment sensitively and give it the importance it deserves. She should be ready to answer tough questions, as well as to deal with the emotional reaction that the child will have. She should understand that this is not about her heartbreak and what she is going through, but instead, about her child and how he will best hear and understand this life-changing news.*

## How to Break the Divorce News to Your Child
### By Rosalind Sedacca, CDC

### Part 1: My Personal Story

I've faced many difficult moments in my life, but preparing to tell my son that I would be divorcing his father was absolutely one of the worst. Thinking about breaking the news filled me with dread, gut-wrenching fear, and incredible guilt. My son, after all, was a sweet, innocent soul who loved both his father and mother. He didn't deserve this.

I struggled with the anxiety for weeks. When should I tell him? How? Should we tell him together? And most frightening of all, *what should we say?*

How do you explain to your child that the life he has known is about to be disrupted—changed—forever?

33

How do you explain that none of this is his fault?

How do you reassure him that life will go on; that he will be safe and loved, even after his parents' divorce?

And, even more intimidating, how do you prepare him for all the unknowns ahead when you're not sure yourself how it will all turn out?

I needed a way of conveying all that I wanted to say to him at a level of understanding that he could grasp.

My son was eleven at the time. He was still a child, yet old enough to feel the tension in our home that had been escalating for several years. He heard the irritation in our voices when his father and I spoke. He heard the arguments that flared up suddenly in the midst of routine conversations and the deafening silence when we were engulfed in our frustration and anger.

Quietly my son was experiencing it all and, not surprisingly, beginning to show signs of stress. Sometimes it came in the form of headaches. Other times his tears revealed his pain at hearing what he heard and being helpless to stop it. Often, he acted out, revealing his escalating temper as he filled up with rage about controlling a situation that was totally beyond his control.

The most frustrating part of all is that my husband and I knew better than to fight in front of our son, allowing him to be caught up in our marital drama. But as our unhappiness grew over time, we lost touch with what we knew and gave in to what we felt. It was a terrible mistake, one which I will always regret because the child I loved more than anyone in the universe was paying the price.

I searched for help online. But while I found suggestions regarding what to say, there was little available on *how to say it.* How do you initiate the most difficult conversation you may ever have with your child—and achieve a positive resolution?

I started by creating a list of what was most important for me to tell my son about the divorce. I honed it down to six points that were most essential:

1. This is not your fault.
2. You are and will always remain safe.
3. Mom and Dad will always be your parents.
4. Mom and Dad will always love you.

5. This is about change, not about blame.
6. Things will work out okay.

I knew this was vital information to get across, but I didn't know how to say it. How do I begin? How do I answer all his questions? How do I cope with the inevitable tears, anger, and pain? And then what?

After weeks of sleepless nights, I awoke at 4 a.m. with a thought that came to me and resonated in a powerful way. I remembered that my son always enjoyed looking through family photo albums, primarily because they were filled with photos of him. He liked seeing his baby pictures and watching the changes as he grew. The albums were like a storybook of his life. They kept his attention and opened the door to many relaxed family conversations.

What if I prepared a photo album for my son that told the story of our family in pictures and words? And what if it spanned from before he was born right up to the present, preparing him for the new changes ahead?

The storybook concept would give him something tangible he could hold on to and read again and again to help him grasp what was about to transpire. It would explain, in language he could understand, why this was happening and would include the six crucial points I knew I had to get across. Rather than rehearsing an awkward conversation, the storybook would give me a written script that was well thought through in advance.

When the book was completed, I showed it to my husband. It was important that we both agreed about the message, which was not controversial, judgmental, or accusatory. It focused on areas of mutual agreement: the six crucial points that almost every parent would want to get across.

While my husband was angry with me for initiating our divorce, he knew the point of our storybook was not to air our differences but to support our son. He agreed the book was well done.

One evening, we sat down with my son and told him we wanted to show him a storybook about our family. He was immediately interested. As I read aloud, I stopped at times to reminisce about a memorable event or occasion. It felt good to laugh together as a family again, even if only briefly.

As I started reading about the changes in our family—the tension and sad times—tears pooled up in my son's eyes. By the time I reached the end, he was weeping uncontrollably and clinging to us both.

Then came the inevitable response. "NO! You're not getting a divorce. I don't want you to. It's not fair." Together, as a family, we talked, cried, hugged, answered questions, re-read passages, and consoled one another.

The deed was done. It was tough to go through, but having the book as an anchor to hold on to and re-read was helpful for us all. We talked about the impending divorce many more times in the following weeks, and even after the divorce itself. Often, we'd refer back to the book as a reminder that Mom and Dad will still love him forever and that everything will be okay.

The book also helped me and my husband keep our son's need in perspective. It reminded us that this was not about judgments and accusations. Life evolves. And beyond our differences, frustrations, and disappointments, we were still both his Mom and Dad and always would be. Therefore, we needed to treat each other with dignity and respect.

It has been more than a decade since I prepared that family storybook. I have since remarried, and my son has embarked on an exciting career as a veterinary cardiologist. As a grown young man, he is still very close to his father and me. When I approached him about sharing my family storybook idea with other parents facing divorce, he enthusiastically agreed it was a great idea.

I can't be more pleased or proud that my son wrote the introduction to my internationally-acclaimed e-book, *How Do I Tell the Kids About the Divorce? A Create-a-Storybook Guide to Preparing Your Children—with Love!* It contains fill-in-the-blank templates that parents can customize about their family. My approach to creating what I call a "child-centered divorce" paid off for us all. It is the crowning achievement in my life.

## PART 2: TELLING YOUR CHILDREN ABOUT THE DIVORCE— AN INNOVATIVE APPROACH THAT'S SENSITIVE AND SANE!

Few children outgrow the warm comfort of a bedtime tale. And like most kids, my son always enjoyed his baby pictures—watching himself grow and change. That idea became the catalyst behind my unusual approach to helping parents break the divorce news to their children. Divorce is certainly no fairytale, but I thought, "Maybe combining a story with our own family photos will help my son grasp the biggest, most dramatic change of his life."

Did our storybook-style divorce explanation take away the pain for our son? Of course not. But I know the tension was reduced significantly. And, through age-appropriate language and photos, it helped us engage him in a way he could understand.

You can use the concepts I've shared here to create a book for your own children.

Or you can use the storybook template in my e-book, featuring advice and suggestions from six different psychotherapists, *How Do I Tell the Kids About the Divorce? A Create-a-Storybook Guide to Preparing Your Children — with Love!* (http://www.howdoitellthekids.com). Either way, the photo storybook approach will be a resource that achieves the following with tenderness and respect:

1. *Puts the divorce in context.* Your divorce is not just the dissolution of your marriage. It's a seismic shift in your family's dynamics. Rather than merely talk about that change, photos help your child visualize it. When we sat our son down, my ex and I talked, cried, hugged, answered his questions, repeated answers, reread passages in the book, and consoled one another. We gave the message that people and situations can change. Life evolves.

2. *Photos provide a natural "script."* I don't know about you, but I felt anxious about rehearsing a how-to-explain-divorce conversation that might leave me open to possible mistakes and detours. We made sure to cover the essentials. But this was the personal story of *our* family. The pictures and text gave us a free flowing yet pre-planned script that was well thought through in advance.

3. *Creates a child-centered focus for parents.* My husband was angry with me for initiating our divorce. Resentment and divorce seem to go hand in hand. Having the book helped us as a couple to keep the perspective on our son. It was a reality check to remind us

that this was not about good guys and bad guys, nor about judgments, accusations, or blame. Beyond our differences, our frustrations, and our disappointments, we were still his mom and dad and always would be. Our son understood that the point of our storybook was not to air our differences but to show him support during this difficult time.

4. *Gives your child a tangible resource.* Kids don't do too well with abstract ideas. Something about the tangible pages of pictures helped our son process the complexity of what our family would soon experience. Sometimes, we'd refer back to a page or two in the book as a reminder that Mom and Dad would love him forever and that everything would be okay.

The conversation about the divorce will come up many, many times in the following weeks and even long after the divorce itself. Referring back to the storybook supports your child's emotional needs, honors his concerns, and reminds him of key messages you want him to grasp.

I'm wishing you great success ahead for everyone in your family during and after the divorce. Always take the high road when making tough decisions. Your children will thank you!

## PART 3: PARENTS BEWARE— SIX DON'TS WHEN DIVORCING WITH CHILDREN!

Are you preparing to break the news to your kids that you and their other parent are getting divorced? Feeling insecure about how to broach the subject? Wondering how much to share during and after the divorce? How your children will react? How to handle their questions? How to deal with your special circumstances? What do the experts suggest?

Well, you're not alone. Talking about divorce to your children is tough. You don't want to make errors you will regret.

There are many common mistakes parents make at this time. Learn six of the most important ones so you can avoid them.

1. *Putting your ex down in front of the kids.* When you speak disrespectfully about your children's other parent, they are often

hurt and riddled with guilt and confusion. Their thinking is, "If there's something wrong with Dad or Mom, there must also be something wrong with me for loving them." This can result in damaging your own relationship with your children as well.

2. *Fighting around the children.* Studies show that conflict is what creates the most pain and turmoil for children of divorce. Keep parental battles away from your children—even when they're sleeping or when you're on the phone. They deserve the peace of mind and will be deeply affected by conflict they can't control or change.

3. *Pressuring children to make choices.* Most kids feel torn when asked to choose between their parents. Don't put them in that position. They can feel very guilty and may not make the decision they prefer in order to protect one or both parents. You can ask for opinions, but don't leave the decisions to your child.

4. *Failing to tell your kids they are not at fault.* Don't assume your children understand that they are victims in your divorce. Remind them frequently that they bear no blame in any way related to your divorce, even and especially if you are fighting with their other parent about them.

5. *Sharing information about which only adults should be aware.* Parents often do this to bond with their children, win their allegiance, or hurt their former spouse. However, it robs them of their childhood and creates an emotional burden that children shouldn't have to bear. Talk to adults about adult issues.

6. *Using your children as spies.* Don't ask or expect your kids to tell you secrets about their other parent's life and home. It makes them feel uncomfortable and puts enormous pressure on them. Don't make your kids your confidants. They'll resent you for it.

Fortunately, you can reach out to many different professionals to help you if you're not positive about how best to approach your children. Speak to a divorce mediator, collaborative attorney, or divorce coach or see a therapist who specializes in this subject. Find an attorney who practices collaborative divorce, which will result in more positive, cooperative outcomes. Seek the advice of parenting coaches, school counselors, clergy, and other professionals. Don't forget the many valuable books and articles on

this          topic.          You'll          find          many          at
http://www.childcentereddivorce.com.

Whatever you do, prepare yourself in advance when talking to your children. Be aware of the impact of your words on their innocent psyches. Avoid the mistakes we have discussed. Think before you leap, and give your family a sound foundation on which to face the changes ahead with security, compassion, and love.

Rosalind Sedacca, CDC, is a divorce and parenting coach, mentor, and founder of the Child-Centered Divorce Network. She's also the author of *How Do I Tell the Kids about the Divorce? A Create-a-Storybook Guide to Preparing Your Children — with Love!* This unique e-book doesn't just tell parents what to say, it provides age-appropriate, customizable templates that *say it for them!*

Ms. Sedacca provides personal telephone coaching services on parenting skills during and after divorce. She also provides digital resources: *Mastering Child-Centered Divorce, a* 10-hour audio coaching program with workbook, as well as her *Parenting Beyond Divorce: Making Life Better for You & Your Children!* training course. Learn more at www.childcentereddivorce.com/coaching-programs.

As host of the *Divorce, Dating & Empowered Living* radio show and podcast, Ms. Sedacca interviews compassionate divorce and relationship experts on crucial topics relevant to parents. She also co-hosted *The Divorce View* talk show and podcast for three years.

Ms. Sedacca is on the faculty of *Divorce Magazine* and is an expert blogger for the *Huffington Post, DivorceForce, Kidz Edge* magazine, *CBS News* "Eye on Parenting," *Exceptional People* magazine, and many of the largest divorce and parenting websites and blogs.

Her www.ChildCenteredDivorce.com blog was selected as the number one blog on the "Best Resources for Divorced Parents and Separated Families" list on the *Radical Parenting* blog.

Ms. Sedacca has also co-authored an eight-hour and 12-hour *Online Anger Management Program for Co-Parents* and high conflict families. http://www.angerconflictprograms.com/

To learn more about Ms. Sedacca's books, services, e-courses, and divorce coaching, visit www.childcentereddivorce.com.

*It's not news to anyone that parenting is hard! Throw a divorce into the mix, and many parents feel inadequate about whether they are protecting their children sufficiently from the negative effects that a separation between the two primary caregivers in their universe can have.*

*Among the many duties of the collaborative coach is teaching the parents how to debrief their children. When a child displays heightened emotions, it is important for the parent to understand what the child is actually communicating. A parent must actively listen and engage with her child so that she hears his true messages. Although these skills can be difficult for the untrained, distressed parent, a mental health professional can coach divorcing parents how to hone these skills. It not only helps build the bond between parent and child but it also teaches the parents communications skills that are helpful in their everyday lives and in their interactions with one another.*

*Learning these skills will help the entire family to transition through divorce in a healthy manner.*

## THE POWER OF PARENTS AS DEBRIEFERS
### BY SUSAN GAMACHE, PH.D., MFT

As a psychologist and licensed marriage and family therapist (AAMFT), I include working as a Collaborative Divorce Coach (CDC) and a Collaborative Child Specialist (CCS) in my practice. In our practice group of approximately 75 members, we work mostly with the two-coach structure from the original Collaborative Divorce model. That is, each parent has a primary relationship with his own divorce coach and a generally supportive relationship with the other divorce coach. The two divorce coaches work jointly as a team and together with the rest of the Collaborative team. This parallels the role of the Collaborative Lawyers, who each provide a non-adversarial advocacy for his client and work as a team with the other lawyer and the other professionals involved.

Often, a Child Specialist and/or a Financial Specialist are also included on the team.

The approach to Collaborative Practice that has evolved in my community is a bit like a toolbox or Lego set. A client may begin with any type of professional (lawyer, mental health, or financial) depending on her unique situation and whom she contacts first. Then, we add the next piece of the team as the client and initial professional feels it is appropriate. Some families use all the tools in the Collaborative Practice toolbox, while others may not.

This can also be considered a family-centric approach in that the family's process and needs are at the center, and the professionals bridge the best of their discipline to the family.[1]

When I work as a CDC or a CCS, my goal is to offer my clients any type of help within my scope of practice that can assist them to reach the best possible outcome for their evolving family. I think of this as their highest level of wellbeing with the minimal level of conflict.[2] Structurally, this can look like one-on-one meetings, four-way meetings (with the other coach and other parent), three-way meetings (with the other coach and the child specialist who has a primary relationship with the children), parent feedback meetings, etc. I also stay connected with all other team members through team meetings. The focus of the teamwork varies to accommodate the capacities and complexities of the family as they navigate the divorce transition.

Parent education has also been a part of my career as a workshop facilitator and as a writer of parent education materials. The task of supporting my clients to learn new parenting skills can fall into the domain of my work as a CDC, as a CCS, or within a general consultation regarding marital transitions from separation through divorce and stepfamily development.

No matter what my job description, one aspect of parent education that frequently comes up is coaching parents to become "debriefers" of their child's experience of the separation.

## Parents as Debriefers

Parents involved in family restructuring often have deep concerns about their children's wellbeing, and rightly so. Parental separation is a serious risk factor in children's lives on many levels. Parents often seek out my services for help with how best to understand their children's needs and to support them through the separation. A central aspect of this work, beyond the *dos and don'ts* of creating a two-household family, is the direct communication between parents and their children as the separation process unfolds, particularly when emotional hotspots arise. Children deliver emotional packages to their parents through their behavior, their language, or their facial expressions. These hotspots or emotional packages create powerful opportunities for parents to connect with their children and to help their children process the strong emotions that parental separation evokes. Parents can be powerful debriefers of their children's experiences of the separation.

During the intensity that often comes with separation, parents can feel overwhelmed or powerless to protect their children from the negative impact of the transition. As children show or tell Mom or Dad something that signals to their parents that they are experiencing confusion, sadness, or any other type of distress, parents often feel emotionally charged themselves and struggle to find effective ways to respond. Developing the skills to effectively capture these moments gives parents confidence and gives children the help they need as they process the emotional aspects of the changes in their family. It also helps to protect and strengthen the parent-child bond, increasing tuned-in-ness and connection.

Parents frequently report situations with their children that I define as emotional hotspots, times when something happened that gave them the experience that their children were upset in some way that was associated with the separation. At these times, I focus on what exactly happened in the situation and what exactly was said:

> What was said in the conversation that unfolded
> when the hotspot arose? What exactly did you say?

> What did your child say? What happened next?
> What did you notice in your child's voice tone, skin
> tone, and/or body language? What did you do?

I find that most parents, while devoted to their children and very well-intentioned, are not that conscious of what exactly they are saying to their children or why. Given that most parents have not been through counseling programs or worked extensively with children other than their own, they are parenting mostly by feel and what feels right. Most of the time, this is good enough.

However, as the separation unfolds, what they generally do may not help them through the hotspots. They don't have a map of this new territory and can feel unsure about what to do. This can be exacerbated by their own strong emotions when they hit an emotional hotspot with their children or when their children deliver an emotional package to them. They can feel angry, sad, scared, or overwhelmed in that moment. They may not even be able to access their usual parenting strengths because of their own upset. (Research on parenting suggests a dip in the quality of parenting in the first year of separation and a return to normal in the second and subsequent years.)

I respond to these types of situations by training parents to become debriefers of their children's experience within the context of their parenting relationship. It is indeed a tall order for a loving parent who is in a period of her own massive change and emotional process around a separation to learn to act as a debriefer for her children. At the same time, the challenge of this task is more than outweighed by the relief a parent feels in finally having a sense of what to do, the immense satisfaction when she gets it right, seeing the positive effect on her children, and experiencing a closer connection with her children through these difficult times.

Some of the responses I hear are:

1. Not saying or doing anything for fear of doing or saying the wrong thing.
2. Feeling so angry or hurt as to freeze up.
3. Asking questions like "What's wrong?" or "How do you feel about that?"

4. Telling the child, "Everything is okay. Don't worry."
5. Telling the child "Don't be silly. It's nothing."
6. Responding, "Yes, but . . . ."

If the child's expression of the emotional hotspot is embedded in problematic behavior, a parent's attempt to limit the behavior or to provide appropriate consequences can backfire making the situation worse. While much of what a parent is doing may be reasonable or good parenting in normal circumstances, there is more she can do in these emotionally heightened times.

## DEBRIEFING CHILDREN THROUGH SEPARATION

### Advanced Parenting Skills

Parenting practices that are generally sufficient for the children in a one-household family may need to be upgraded to fit the two-household family. Although it may be a relief for the parents to no longer be parenting together, parenting in a two-household family can also have its challenges. Single parents are generally overwhelmed with tasks with little backup. Parents no longer witness each other's parenting, so trusting that the children are well cared for may be more difficult. There is, by definition, emotional disruption in the family as well as many tasks that must be accomplished to complete the separation. There is also less time with the children and a smaller margin of error.

### "Fix-It" Mode

When parents hit an emotional hotspot with their children around the separation, the typical response is to go into "fix-it" mode. As parents, we want to do something to fix the problem; make the pain, sadness, anxiety, or distress go away. Unfortunately, in the separation process, parents cannot make it all go away. While parents can do their best to buffer their children from the stress of the separation, it is impossible to protect children from everything. In addition, children have their own feelings about the separation and have the right to feel these feelings as the transition unfolds.

Parents can feel helpless, hopeless, angry, and confused when they do not feel sure about what to do. Going into "fix-it" mode can be the natural reflex.

## Parents as Debriefers

Learning how to be a debriefer for their children does not negate everything else parents do. It is a skill to use when they hit the emotional hotspot or receive the emotional package from a child that signals to his parent that he is in an emotionally heightened or charged state. The emotional package can come to the parent as a statement about the separation, a behavior, or the absence of something the parent understands to be normal. The parent experiences a heightening of emotion when she receives the emotional package. This signals to the parent that the child is communicating something beyond the everyday that is likely associated with the family changes. Once the parent has received and dealt with the emotional package, she can go back to her regular parenting practices.

## Metaphors

The process of being a parent debriefer can be described with metaphors that help parents to have an intuitive sense of the whole. Metaphors I commonly use are: treading water; massaging the moment; sitting with; expanding the moment; putting yourself in their shoes; and turning into a mirror.

## Making the Shift

In order to help parents understand the shift in perspective of this different role, sometimes I change my place in the consultation room. I leave my chair, which is generally facing them, and sit or kneel right beside them. I explain that when you shift to the posture of the debriefer, it is as if you are coming right beside your child to do your best to see it how they see it, to feel it as they feel it. There is no judgment or blame, just gentle curiosity. While it is not always necessary to actually change your place in relation to your child when acting as a parent debriefer, making the mental shift is the first step.

The purpose is for the parent to assist the child to go *more* into his own experience and to teach his parent *more* about what is happening for him. This may be counter to some parents' reflexes to avoid the feelings or to encourage their children to suppress them. Just how is the child putting this all together for himself in his own way at his place in his development? Given that a child's brain does not have the same cognitive ability as his parents', his way of understanding the situation will be different than what his parents can imagine a lot of the time. Who can remember how the world looked to us when we were five, ten, or 15 years old?[3]

Example: "Oh, hmmm, so when you think of going to camp, it looks unfair because Fluffy can't come with you. Fluffy might be sad to be at home without you."

## A Note on Noticing

Noticing is a very powerful tool for parents at any time. When noticing is a part of parenting practices, it creates a gentle connection that communicates to a child that he matters. Noticing is not difficult. It involves the parent simply letting the child know that she has noticed him or something about him. It can be light, quick, and brief. Noticing communicates, "I see you, I notice you, I care, you matter." When a child knows that his parent notices him without him having to get her attention, it gives him a sense of security and comfort and lets him know she is tuned-in with him.

Example: "You sure do a good job of taking care of Fluffy. Fluffy is so lucky."

## Advanced Listening

I teach parents to think of each interaction with their children as 100%, no matter how long or short it is. I then ask them to frontload their listening, to consider leaving the "parent as fixer" for the last 20%, and consider using the "parent as debriefer" for the first 80%. This means using advanced listening skills first to learn more about what their child is actually saying to them before crafting a next step or solution.

Once they have used the "parent as debriefer" skills, they will know much more about what their child is experiencing. Then, in the remaining 20%, parents can return to "parent as fixer" and work to find solutions that take into consideration much more accurate information about what would be helpful. In addition, the child will have experienced a connection and tuned-in-ness with his parent that, in and of itself, is very soothing and helpful. He will also have learned some new ways to communicate about feelings that will increase his own ability to communicate about his own experience.

## Making the Shift

Shifting gears to "parent as debriefer" starts with hitting the pause button. Parents learn to pause their usual reaction and shift into debriefer mode. This means stopping what they are doing and temporarily putting the world of adult affairs on hold. At the beginning, this may require a lot of concentration, so it may not be possible when driving or otherwise occupied in activities that cannot be put on hold. At these times, the parent can let the child know that she heard him and will get back to him about that as soon as she can, hopefully in the next few minutes, or at the very latest, that same day. Once these skills are more integrated, they will feel more natural and be accessible in the midst of other things.

*The parent must give the child her full attention.* She should put down what she is doing. Refrain from texting or computer use. Stop cooking for a moment. It may also mean shifting physically into a posture that is closer to the child or going down on one knee to be more at eye level with a young child.

## Paraphrasing

Paraphrasing means saying again what the child has said but in similar or different words. While this may sound either innocuous or patronizing, when done well, it is a very powerful tool for the parent debriefer.

*Speak slowly.* When paraphrasing, it is important to slow down. As emotions get heightened, conversations often speed up. Just the act of slowing down a conversation helps the emotions to calm and clarify.

*Voice tone.* When a parent understands the statement or behavior to be an emotional package, it is easy to see that loud voices will not help. The parent should use a neutral, soft tone of voice.

*Identify the emotion in the package.* The parent should try to identify the emotion in the package that has just been delivered to her. Keep it simple. Sad, mad, scared, confused, frustrated?

Example:

> (Child looking sad and worried) "Fluffy won't have anywhere to sleep in the apartment!"

> (You, down on one knee, slowly, gently) "You are worried about where Fluffy will sleep in our new home."

*Stop and wait.* The parent's statement has just opened the door for her child to tell her more about his concerns. A moment of quiet lets him know that she is interested in what he has to say and is making the time to listen to him. It also communicates love and respect for him. Paraphrasing offers a child the opportunity to learn the emotion words that go with how he is feeling. It may take him a moment or two to digest these words and figure out what he wants to say back.

Emotion takes time to process. In order to process emotion, children (and parents) need time for things to sink in and to resurface in words. It's a little like diving down and coming back up to the surface. It could be a shallow dive or a deeper one. I imagine emotional process as going on underwater in contrast to thinking that takes place on land. We can start, stop, and turn quickly on land, but it is much slower underwater. We need to give some extra time to allow the meanings of things to become clear.

Example:

> (Child, on the verge of tears) "You said we can't take her bed because it is too big."

> (You, slowly, thoughtfully) "Oh, so you want Fluffy to have as nice a bed in our new place as she has here.

> (Child, brightening to a smile) "Yes, she can sleep in my room!" (Clearly the answer he has already thought about.)

*Non-verbal behavior.* When paraphrasing, parents can learn to notice their child's non-verbal behavior as well as what he says. I teach them to watch body language, tear lines in the eye, skin tone changes on his cheeks or neck, changes of position, sighing etc. All these signs give information to parents about the effectiveness of their statement to connect with their child's experience. In the world of family therapy, we call this the "recognition reflex." In poker, it is called the "tell."

*The trouble with questions.* Every parent asks their child questions, and under normal circumstances, questions are a useful part of communication. At the same time, when a child is in an emotionally-charged state during parental separation, questions are often not helpful. It can be tempting for a parent to use questions to try to better understand her child's experience. In some situations, this will be fine. However, during a separation, a child can become reluctant to say things he feels might upset his parent or may not know how to articulate the complex emotions he is feeling. Sometimes he worries about talking about what happened in the other household.

To understand how questions can be tricky, consider them like arrows—they have a direction and a point. Given that we are adults, we will not be experiencing things as our child does, so our direction may not be the one that fits with him. Also, a question demands an answer. If the question is not helpful, then the child has the problem of how to "not answer" the question and so may just not know what to say. This may have the effect of shutting down the very conversation the parent is trying to encourage.

*Paraphrasing statements are non-directional.* Paraphrasing statements do not direct conversations. They are conversational treading water that stays in one place. They are "non-demand" statements. "You sound sad." "Gosh, you are really thinking a lot about that." "That sounds very important to you." An answer is not required.

*Getting it wrong.* When paraphrasing, it is not a problem to be wrong. If a parent is off the mark in her attempt to paraphrase, there is no harm done. As the parent is corrected by her child, she has still succeeded in creating a conversational connection that supports the child's experience of being heard, respected, and loved. Even better, the child is now engaged in the conversation to make the correction and improve the quality of the parent's understanding.

*Expanding the moment.* Paraphrasing expands the moment to allow more information to surface and to be expressed. Everyone wins when the emotional package a child delivers is unpacked. It then becomes a doorway that can open up to create greater connection, respect, and more accurate understanding.

*It's about him.* Fundamentally, paraphrasing takes the parent's emotional experience out of the mix for the moment, turning the parent into a mirror for the child's experience. This allows the conversation to focus entirely on the child. This can give a parent time to catch her breath if the child's emotional package has caused her upset. "Daddy says you don't want to be part of the family anymore." "I hate living in two houses." In these cases, staying with the child's experience may offer a parent some time to catch her breath and to avoid engaging the child in the adult issues.

## Beyond Paraphrasing

If a paraphrasing statement did not elicit a response, the parent can let it go or continue. If the parent lets it go, the child still receives the benefit of her attention and her positive intention to be available to him. He also hears the language that, rightly or wrongly, she is using to describe what she believes is going on for him. This supports trust and safety and the possibility of communication in the future. He may come back to her later with this idea or respond next time she offers it.

Here are a few ideas that go well with paraphrasing and may allow parents to go a little further:

1. To continue in the conversation, try wondering. "I'm wondering" is a lot like asking a question without the demand for an answer. You can communicate what you are curious about and just let the statement float in the air. For example, "Hmmm, I wonder what would help Fluffy feel more comfortable in the apartment." This is a non-demand statement because it does not demand an answer. It floats and can be engaged with or not.

2. Another way for a parent to keep going if her child is not responding is to share what it might be like for her. For example, "Hmmm, (slowly), if I was Fluffy, and I was feeling worried about the move, I might feel batter knowing that my bed will be near your bed."

3. Acknowledging he doesn't want to talk about it right now notices where a child is emotionally without putting pressure on him to speak. Putting pressure on him can inadvertently make it less likely that he will share his thoughts and feelings with his parent. Framing it as not wanting to talk about it "right now," also suggests that he may want to talk about it later. For example, "Hmm, looks like maybe you don't want to talk about this right now. How about some dessert?" And let it go.

4. The language of wishing can help give a parent a way to express to a child what she wishes she could change but cannot.[4] One client of mine, an architect, used this effectively to address his children's sadness about having to be with him in a small apartment. Here are his comments about using the language of wishing:

> Our two girls, then aged 9 and 7, often criticized me for the considerable decline in our lifestyle following the separation. Instead of refuting the children's views, I would share with them my wishes for better things, such as having our own home or travelling to exotic cities together as in

the past. As an architect, I have even shared my wishful sketches of the perfect family home for the girls and me. This let the children know that I hear them and share some of their wishes. It also shows them I also have high hopes for the future without involving them in adult issues like finances.

## Columbo

For those of us old enough to have enjoyed Peter Falk in this well-loved television detective show, the character of Lieutenant Columbo can be another very useful way to help our clients get a sense of the voice of the debriefer. For those who did not grow up with this show, it is easily available on YouTube.

Columbo was a detective who mastered the art of interviewing in a unique way. I call this being "dumb like a fox." Lieutenant Columbo always seemed a little confused, dim-witted or forgetful, and very self-deprecating. But we all knew that he was doing everything exactly as he wanted and was in complete control of the situation. In the family therapy world, we call this the "one down position." We do not make statements that communicate dominance, but rather approach a situation with bemused curiosity. This voice tone can support paraphrasing and wondering, as well as the other aspects of paraphrasing described above.

Columbo did a lot of paraphrasing and wondering. But perhaps his most interesting technique was "the crazy idea." This gave him, and can give separating parents, permission to mindread (or at least to try to mindread) without worrying about not getting it quite right. A parent may not know everything her child is experiencing, but often she has a pretty good idea of what her child is thinking. When a parent is acting as a debriefer, she can use "the crazy idea" to express her best guess about what her child is thinking without creating a demand for a response. Once we state that we have a crazy idea, we can say almost anything. Right or wrong, the parent will also get some good non-verbal information from her child through the recognition reflex as the statement is launched and her child receives it.

One of my parents called "the crazy idea" a game changer in his relationship with his seven-year-old:

> You know, I have this crazy idea, probably completely wrong, that maybe you were thinking that we might not be taking good enough care of Fluffy as our family moves into two homes. And, I don't know, but maybe you have been thinking about it and have some ideas of your own about how we can take better care of Fluffy.

Here is a description by one dad of his experience with the Columbo idea:

> Columbo's inquisitive, half-wit approach allows me to disarm the children and yet suggest thoughts and reasons for their behavior, which otherwise may become exacerbated. Now 13 and 11 years old, the girls, as well as the separation conflict, have settled considerably, but I still use the technique. The girls often mimic me for the "Columbo" technique, which remains one of the best tools in my parenting toolbox.

### "Why Are You Talking Funny?"

Some children will notice the difference in how their parents are speaking to them. "Why are you talking so funny? Stop talking like that." A parent can respond, "Because I love you so much, I am learning new ways to communicate to help everyone through the separation process." Children generally accept this way of speaking ultimately because it feels so good.

Exaggerating to the point of ridiculousness can also help children understand that using these communication practices is not menacing or threatening.

Example: "I wish we could live at Disneyland all the time and have dinner every night with Snow White and the Seven Dwarves and Cinderella and Peter Pan and even the Wicked Witch!"

## COACHING PARENTS TO BE DEBRIEFERS

### Role-Play as a Teaching Tool

For some people, role-play is about as interesting as a root canal. However, it is a great teaching tool with parents. As a parent describes the impossible situation with her child, it is generally clear that her responses, as well-intentioned as they are, are not helping. I invite her to play the role of her child in the situation she is describing, and I take on the role as the parent debriefer. This seems to be an acceptable way to enter into a role-play even for the most resistant because she gets the easier role.

Building on her description of what's not working, a parent can usually play the role of her child quite easily. It often seems like a relief to not have to figure out what to do. Generally, we just have a few exchanges before my client has no idea what her child would say. So I ask her to guess. She knows more than she thinks she knows, so I ask her to just make it up. Even if she is not exactly accurate, this gives us material and opportunity to use different skills, practice voice tone, and develop some crazy ideas. I love watching a parent's face light up when she realizes that she has all kinds of ideas about what is going on for her child, and now she has a way to communicate that effectively without being invasive or confrontational.

I also encourage humor by exaggerating an aspect that might make her child laugh. For example, "I just have this crazy idea that maybe Fluffy really wants your bed and pink PJs just like yours!"

### The Apology

During "parents as debriefer" conversations, a child sometimes shares painful experiences, and a parent can feel guilt or remorse for the separation, whether or not she is the initiator. In these moments, an apology (without blame) can be a very loving response to a child. For example, "I am so sorry that our family is going through this. This is not what we thought would ever happen in our family. I love you so much, and I'm sorry that this is happening."

Sharing the sadness of the separation can help a child know that it is normal to feel sad, that other people in the family feel sad, and that feeling his sadness can help it diminish.

## CONCLUSION

Although unintended, the separation process provides an opportunity to learn new parenting practices that will serve parents and children well past the establishing of a two-home family. These skills can become a part of the restructured family's parenting culture and can help deal with anything that comes the parents' way in the future.

For parents with children who are delivering emotional packages that are overwhelming or who are continually running into hotspots, a collaborative divorce coach or child specialist can coach parents in these and other skills that can greatly assist them to move through the separation transition more smoothly. It may also be helpful for children to spend time with a child specialist or child counselor to give them a supportive and neutral place to express their experiences of the separation.

For more information, please see the following:

Gamache, S. (2015). Family Peacemaking with an Interdisciplinary Team: A Therapist's Perspective. *Family Court Review*, Vol. 53 (3) 378 – 387.

Gamache, S. (2013). Locating and Defining Divorce Coaching for the Family Therapist. The Collaborative Review; Journal of the International Academy of Collaborative Professionals 13(1).

Gamache, S. (2004). The Role of the Divorce Coach. In N. J. Cameron Collaborative Practice: Deepening the Dialogue. Continuing Legal Education, British Columbia.

Gamache, S. (2004). The Role of the Child Specialist. In N. J. Cameron Collaborative Practice: Deepening the Dialogue. Continuing Legal Education, British Columbia.

[1] Gamache, S. (2015) Family Peacemaking with an Interdisciplinary Team: A Therapist's Perspective. Family Court Review Vol. 53 (3) 378 – 387.

[2] Gamache, S. (2013) *Collaborative Divorce Coaching; Working toward A Definition and Theoretical Location for the Family Therapist.*

[3] Siegel, D. & Bryson, T., (2012). *The Whole Brain Child; 12 Revolutionary Strategies to Nurture Your Childs Developing Mind.*

[4] Faber, A. & Mazlish, E. (2006). *How to Talk So Kids Will Listen and Listen So Kids Will Talk.* Scribner Classics.

Susan Gamache, Ph.D., MFT, has made the development of collaborative practice a central focus in her career since 1999. She is a psychologist and licensed marriage and family therapist in private practice in Vancouver, Canada. She is also a mediator, parent educator, media consultant, and writer.

In addition to general practice with individuals, couples, and families, Dr. Gamache has dedicated her practice to helping children and families through separation, divorce, and remarriage.

She was awarded the President's Award for Contributions and Advocacy for Families by the BC Association of Registered Clinical Counselors for her work in this area and the Randy Gerson Award for Advancement in Family Systems by the American Psychological Association for her graduate research.

Dr. Gamache acted as first mental health co-chair of the Collaborative Divorce Vancouver Collaborative Group (1999–2003), board member of IACP (2003–2006), and returned to the Vancouver Executive (2010 to 2014). During this time, she was also the mental health chair of the annual provincial training in CP for continuing legal education in British Columbia, a training that won the ACLEA award for Best Program the year it was introduced.

An active participant in CP files as a collaborative divorce coach and child specialist, she has also provided over 70 presentations/trainings in seven countries on CP, has authored 15 publications on CP, and has presented at 12 IACP networking forums since 2002 and three European collaborative conferences. Dr. Gamache has co-taught three full credit courses on interdisciplinary collaborative practice in the faculty of law at UBC.

Over the past two years, she has built on the original collaborative divorce model to create REACH, a therapeutic team approach that includes senior legal and therapeutic practitioners working in an integrated model to help court-involved families experiencing alienation, high conflict, and/or problems of high complexity.

Dr. Gamache provides training on separation and divorce for organizations of psychological professionals. She was a board member and trainer for the Stepfamily Association of America (1995–2000). Throughout her graduate work, Dr. Gamache studied children and families moving through separation, divorce, and remarriage, as well as facilitated workshops for parents living through these transitions.

Over the past 20 years, Dr. Gamache has continued to build on a keynote address for professionals and the public that examines the history and current role of divorce in today's society and the evolving social and cultural practices that maintain it.

*While some strive for perfection in their careers and lives, setting such unrealistic goals can be a recipe for disaster. If unable to face the inevitability that mistakes happen, an individual will not allow himself to take risks that could lead to amazing results. He will never have the opportunity to be truly great if he is unwilling to take calculated chances.*

*Further, an individual who endeavors to be perfect will not be content with his colleagues who set more realistic goals for themselves and for their teammates. Collaborative professionals will be less than willing to include perfectionists on their teams for fear of constantly letting them down or concern that their every move is being judged.*

*Although a person with a tendency toward perfectionism can be a valuable asset to a collaborative team because of his attention to detail, if too much focus is placed on being perfect, the team will suffer. Impasse will be more likely because there is no such thing as a perfect agreement.*

*Rather than seeking perfection in yourself and your colleagues, lower your expectations just a bit, and you'll contribute more to the team and find more happiness within yourself.*

## How MHPs Build Relationships
## to Become a Part of the Team
### By Julia A. McAninch, Psy.D.

Mental health professionals are well trained on how to establish relationships with clients by building rapport, creating trust, and learning and adjusting to their clients' needs. In the psychotherapeutic relationship, there is a power differential that most clinicians are also taught to acknowledge and navigate with sensitivity given that the MHP is in a unique position to influence their[1] clients' lives. There is a natural transition from the therapist role to the collaborative divorce coach role with the clients, especially if the MHP has been practicing relationship and family therapy. There is a clear understanding of the vital importance of the relationship with the client and the impact that relationship has on creating positive change.

However, MHPs rarely receive direct training in how to establish relationships with their professional colleagues. While MHPs do work with treatment teams when functioning as therapists, they do so with less frequent contact and interreliance on one another than is required from participation on a collaborative team. Frequently, new CDCs report feeling disempowered in their role with their new colleagues, attorneys, and financial professionals who they perceive, sometimes rightly so, as having more of a voice and role in the divorce process than the MHP. This experience can lead CDCs to an unfamiliar place of being unsure of how to best serve their clients and the collaborative divorce process.

Strong relationships and trust amongst the collaborative team are pivotal to the success of the process for the clients. The team provides a safe holding environment for the clients and their family while they engage in a major life transition. However, the team cannot be a safe holding environment if they are not attending to the relationships between the team members. The more unsettled and disjointed the team relationships, the less steady the boat will feel for the clients during their personal storms.

So how do CDCs begin to develop strong relationships with their colleagues to provide this safe holding environment? By being a good enough colleague. The "good enough parent" was initially developed by Donald Winnicott and then broadened in its definition and application by later theorists. A recent article by Dr. Peter Gray (2015) reflected on some of the aspects of "good enough parenting" that are applicable to being a good enough colleague.[2]

One aspect of the good enough colleague is that they know, with a grounded confidence, that they are a good enough colleague. They don't feel the pressure to overcompensate or hide in their role, which can easily lead to over and under-functioning CDCs. They approach their colleagues with an awareness that they will work together to figure out this new relationship and process together. That level of presence may seem daunting to achieve, especially fresh out of the gate. But it can be more easily obtained when remembering a few key components of the good enough colleague.

Good enough colleagues do not expect themselves or others to be perfect. When perfection is the goal or feels necessary to be seen as qualified to sit at the table with colleagues, then every mistake will feel insurmountable and can lead to more restricted interactions out of fear of making mistakes. The CDC should model that mistakes happen and that everyone has imperfections, but they can make amends, correct course, and heal the relationship. This is not only powerful for team cohesion, but also for the family who needs this message during a divorce more than at any other time in their lives.

Good enough colleagues recognize and tolerate differences between themselves and their colleagues. Differences can bring about creative ideas and an opportunity to more intimately get to know and understand each other. In new relationships, differences can feel scary because there is uncertainty around how conflict will be navigated and if it will be navigated successfully. The CDC is often looked to as a guide in moments of difference between team members which provides a great opportunity to guide discussion, create communication norms, and breathe through the moments of impasse with a non-anxious energy that generates confidence and trust. A CDC can also deepen intimacy by showing curiosity about the diverse perspectives of their colleagues, which in turn facilitates getting to know one another better.

A CDC who is channeling the good enough colleague will also be able to recognize that the clients and their colleagues are responsible for their own choices. That perspective creates space for the collaborative team to be a guiding force instead of an imposing one. By recognizing the clients' and their colleagues' abilities to make sound decisions and have their own journeys, the CDC becomes less anxious and imposing toward the clients and their colleagues because they have a right-sized perspective about everyone's roles. The good enough colleague recognizes that the best the team can do with each other is to provide the best conditions for the clients to live into their capacities to make solid decisions in their divorce. The impact this has on the collegial relationship is that it decreases the pressure, anxiety, and friction between the collaborative team and creates an open space for self-discovery and self-definition.

Good enough colleagues support one another without dominating each other. This balance may look like a colleague struggling with their relationship with a client. Rather than the CDC dictating how their colleague should act, they support the colleague's exploration of the relationship with the client and what may be problematic in the moment. This approach does not mean that the good enough colleague never becomes directive or assertive—quite the opposite. The good enough colleague knows when a stronger intervention may be needed with a colleague, and the CDC then steps into that space with respect and care. The good enough colleague will also know when to give a colleague more space in their process and not over-function. The natural ebb and flow in the support colleagues need from each other takes practice and open communication.

The most important skills that a good enough colleague brings to their relationships with the team of professionals are self-reflection, empathy, and authenticity. These skills allow relationships to breathe and grow in an ever-changing context of conflict within and around the team. A CDC who can practice healthy feedback (through observation, self-reflection, sharing, and integration) will gain the trust and respect of their colleagues much more quickly.

Being a good enough colleague is challenging work that requires vulnerability. But it can lead to tremendous rewards. Not only will the quality of the collaborative divorce work improve and provide greater support for families, but the richness of the collegial relationships will be sustaining throughout the CDC's career.

---

[1] Pronouns have been adapted to be gender neutral to be inclusive of diverse identities.

[2] Gray (2015, Dec., 22), *The Good Enough Parent is the Best Parent*. Retrieved from Psychology Today at https://www.psychologytoday.com/blog/freedom-learn/201512/the-good-enough-parent-is-the-best-parent.

Julia A. McAninch, Psy.D., is a licensed psychologist providing therapy for individuals, relationships, families, and groups. She is also a Rule 31 listed mediator. She is president of McAninch Psychological & Consulting Services, PLLC (MPCS).

Dr. McAninch was a founding board member of the Middle Tennessee Collaborative Alliance (MTCA). She has served as president and vice president, helping to establish the role of the collaborative divorce coach in Tennessee. She is a graduate of the Inaugural Leadership Academy of the International Academy of Collaborative Professionals (IACP).

One of Dr. McAninch's passions is training. She has conducted numerous trainings on a wide range of topics and is a national trainer with the Interdisciplinary Collaborative Divorce Trainers (ICDT).

An advocate for multicultural concerns and a consultant on leadership and organizational development, Dr. McAninch has worked with practice groups, academic institutions, and organizations. Having served on numerous non-profit boards, she is particularly proud of being a founding board member of one of the first LGBTQ community centers in Tennessee, OutCentral. She is also a past co-chair and on the Advisory Council of the Nashville Psychotherapy Institute (NPI), an organization comprised of 400 mental health professionals throughout middle Tennessee. Dr. McAninch has been an adjunct professor at Vanderbilt University and Columbia College Chicago, and she is a frequent guest lecturer.

*Because collaborative practice is a relatively emerging method, it can be challenging for professionals to shift seamlessly from their former, often combative, practice styles to the more peaceful, holistic methods utilized by collaborative practitioners. An aggressive litigator may have a hard time refraining from arguing what might happen in court. He may find it difficult to speak to the other spouse as a friend rather than as an opponent. He may not seem to fully grasp the concept of transparency. Practitioners with many years of experience behind them may find it even more difficult because they have been practicing a certain way for so long, and collaborative practice is radically different. Many collaborative professionals find themselves slipping back into their old tendencies, much to the chagrin of their collaborative teammates.*

*The paradigm shift can be especially difficult for practitioners who do not transition to full alternative dispute resolution practices, and instead, bounce back and forth between very different practice styles. Understandably, it is difficult to transition frequently between litigator and peacemaker.*

*Why can professionals have such a hard time making the paradigm shift, and what do you do if you notice that a teammate is having a hard time?*

## WOLF IN SHEEP'S CLOTHING: WHY IT'S DIFFICULT FOR COLLABORATIVE PROFESSIONALS TO MAKE THAT "PARADIGM SHIFT" AND WHAT TO DO IF THEY DON'T![1]
### BY LANA M. STERN, PH.D.

The collaborative process requires a significant change in how its participants conduct themselves during a divorce negotiation. This new perspective, known in the field as the "paradigm shift," is the goal of the professionals and our hope for the divorcing couple. This shift involves a fundamental change in how the spouses and the professionals think, feel, act, and speak during the process. It is a difficult transition to master and must ultimately become internalized as part of each individual's persona. It is understandably challenging for the professionals, who have successfully used specific skills in their various practices before becoming collaborative, to change their *habits* and to now engage in a very different way of interacting. Becoming a collaborative professional requires a willingness to master new skills and an openness to using alternative methods of resolving conflict.

Professionals who train in the collaborative process are sincere and curious about how divorce can be less contentious. But once a commitment to practice collaboratively has been made, there are many instances in which the professionals fall back into old habits. What accounts for these relapses? What makes staying collaborative so challenging? Why do well-meaning collaboratively trained professionals suffer from these slips? And, most importantly, what can the collaborative team do when they occur?

## COGNITIVE DISSONANCE AND REGRESSION

In one of my recent collaborative cases, the husband's attorney continued to add provisions to the marital settlement agreement that his client did not request. He transmitted these additional stipulations by a formal letter to the other attorney, without discussing them or their impact with the clients and team. The second attorney was now obligated to notify his client about these changes. As the mental health professional on the team, I was not copied on these communications and was only alerted when the second attorney, and later the couple, called to discuss the matter. The result was distressing to the couple, who had already agreed to legal terms and was moving into an emotional closure. This old habit of the lawyer caused an argument between them—each blamed the other for changing their agreement.

What happened? The husband's attorney had regressed into litigation mode. One reason why professionals may not be able to remain collaborative is the internal struggle that results when several conflicting values arise at a critical moment. This occurrence, known as "cognitive dissonance," can cause anxiety and discomfort when a person is confronted with contradictory standards. These conflicts can cause significant discomfort; the person often copes by reverting to older, more familiar ways of operating.

For attorneys, the internal conflict is precipitated by the differing values of the adversarial litigator to the collaborative advisor. Many years of practice have ingrained in most attorneys a focused objective of obtaining the maximum financial outcome for their clients. In the collaborative process, the clients are an active part of the process and can voice what is most important to them in determining their own futures; this may conflict with the attorney's traditional concept of "winning."

There are other issues for the attorneys. They normally operate under the "authority" of the law and within the procedural rules of court. In the collaborative process, the team relies on honesty and transparency from both the clients and the other attorney to produce important documents and information.

This reliance can be especially difficult for the attorney when there is a power imbalance between the clients in terms of their knowledge of business and finances. What happens if the clients are not interested in documents the legal process usually requires? What are the attorneys' responsibilities *then*? Are they subject to potential malpractice claims if evidence is not obtained and preserved?

For the MHP, changes are complex as well. Psychotherapy is typically a confidential relationship with an individual, couple, or family in a series of private meetings. But the collaborative process is a transparent interaction involving the sharing of information with the entire team. Additionally, MHPs can be tasked with the unfamiliar role of facilitating the team dynamics, which can consist of leading team meetings, conducting "debriefings," and monitoring the "collaborative behavior" of all participants. These changes and responsibilities may be beyond the comfort zone of many MHPs.

In a traditional litigation case, the financial professional is retained as an expert witness for one side to support a particular interpretation of financial issues. He is involved in the discovery process, determining the parties' income and lifestyle, calculating tax effects of asset allocation, and devising various schedules of spousal and child support. In contrast, in the collaborative process, the FP plays a neutral role, performing many of the same analyses, but doing so with the participation of both clients. The scope of disclosure is determined by the clients. This can create significant discomfort for the FPs, who may now be limited in advising and persuading clients toward particular outcomes. What if more documents are needed for a comprehensive review but the clients are unwilling to authorize? Are FPs held to the standard of "due diligence?" Do the same liability issues apply to the FPs as they do to the attorneys?

The collaborative process utilizes new rules, concepts, and expectations for all involved. This environment can generate internal tension for the professionals and their clients. When this tension is sustained over time, especially under duress in emotionally charged interactions, it is easy for the professional and the couple to regress to earlier, more familiar patterns of behavior. It is often at these times that collaborative professionals will be charged with "not acting collaboratively."

Examples of non-collaborative behavior include:

- Direct attorney/attorney negotiations without involving the entire team;
- Disempowerment of the clients by excluding them from the decision-making process;
- Repartee of positional posturing by withholding information for strategic gain;
- Use or misuse of emails that inflame the process;
- Use of a formal letter sent to "certify" an issue;
- Lack of inclusion of the MHP and FP in all aspects of the process;
- Employing the courtroom strategy, "Don't ask for permission, ask for forgiveness;"
- The MHP lapsing into therapeutic interventions instead of facilitating the process;
- Loss of neutrality by the MHP;

- Loss of neutrality by the FP;
- The FP preparing equitable distribution charts and alimony schedules without client input;
- The FP addressing only the moneyed or powerful spouse;
- Elimination of pre/post team meetings;
- Minimizing the importance of employing the debrief; and
- Failing to use a full team model.

## TRANSFERENCE/COUNTER-TRANSFERENCE

Another threat to the maintenance of the collaborative mindset comes from two closely related psychological processes called "transference" and "counter-transference." Transference is an unconscious projection of one's own feelings, conflicts, or attitudes (positive or negative) onto a current person, situation, or circumstance. Counter-transference is the reverse, when the other person projects their feelings, conflicts, or attitudes back toward the other party. These projections can account for instant bonding with or hostility toward a new person or situation. When they occur, inaccurate interpretations and expectations of the situation and process can develop.

Examples of transference in the collaborative paradigm include:

- Strong emotional feelings (positive or negative) by the client toward an attorney or another member of the team;
- Unrealistic expectations about the depth of the relationship with the attorney or another team member;
- Dependency on an attorney, MHP, or FP as decision-maker, protector, or savior; and
- Transfer of anger or blame from a client to the spouse's attorney or to another member of the team.

Examples of counter-transference in the team framework include:

- Over-identification by the attorney or another team member with the client and/or the client's issues;

73

- Strong feelings by the attorney or another team member (positive or negative) toward the client;
- Strong feelings by the attorney or another team member (positive or negative) toward another member of the team;
- Disclosure of too much personal information to the client;
- Special "favors" or treatment not usually given to a client or other team member;
- Feeling the need to protect, rationalize, or excuse the behavior of a client or another team member; and
- Taking sides with the client against the other spouse and their attorney.

The transference/counter-transference dynamic and one's immediate personal problems can sometimes intrude into professional work. In one of my more demanding collaborative cases, the attorney representing the husband coincidently was also going through his own difficult divorce. He identified with the husband's trauma and with the husband's description of the wife's behavior. It soon became obvious that he was confusing the dynamics of the collaborative divorce with his own personal situation. In the team meeting, his body language and verbal comments directed toward the wife were disproportionately hostile; he attributed qualities and actions to her that had no basis in fact. He insinuated that she was a "liar" and that she was "not fit" to parent the children without any evidence to support his claim. Transference/counter-transference within the professional team prevented collaboration for the clients.

## "BATTLE SCARS"

Yet another impediment to remaining collaborative could well be titled "battle scars." Attorney-attorney dynamics (and attorney-FP dynamics) can obviously have a significant impact over years of prior relationship in the working environment of the process. Many attorneys and FPs involved in a given collaborative case have litigated against each other previously and/or know each other's reputations. There may be positive or negative histories, alliances, or trust issues between old adversaries. Memories of previous courtroom skirmishes can seriously affect the interaction between the attorneys, creating transference/counter-transference issues. Similarly, experiences with the given FP in prior cases can generate the same dynamics. Examples include:

- Withholding of necessary documents or information to the team based on a recent case, reputation, or other personal interactions;
- Formal correspondence between the attorneys to "memorialize" an issue;
- Refusal to negotiate without a "global settlement package;" and
- Refusal to participate in planned pre/post team meetings or debriefs.

Consider a scenario in which two prominent attorneys in town are old rivals. They are well matched and have a long history of competitive, high profile litigious trials over many years. They know each other's strategies, tricks, and moves. Both have now become collaboratively trained and have demonstrated their commitment by attending many advanced collaborative workshops. When paired with other collaborative attorneys, they adhere to the principals of true collaboration and cooperation. However, when paired with each other in a collaborative case, they may "talk the talk" of collaboration but they definitely do not "walk the walk." They are like two old generals meeting and preparing for battle—collaboration becomes the casualty.

Professionals must learn to self-regulate their emotional reactions when paired in a collaborative divorce with an old adversary. One power of the team is that it can perform checks and balances to keep old rivals apprised of any non-collaborative behavior. The debriefing component of the collaborative process serves as an effective mechanism for this input.

## PARALLEL PROCESS

Parallel process emerges when the professionals unintentionally recreate and act out the conflict of their clients. This dynamic is mostly observed in highly litigated cases, but it can appear in the collaborative setting, as well. The attorneys identify with their clients and act out the hostile, emotional struggles between them. Often, the personal wishes of the couple are overlooked as the battling attorneys become preoccupied with their personal agenda.

In a very difficult gray divorce case involving a forty-year marriage, infidelities, lack of trust between the spouses, and a lifestyle that had depleted their savings, one of the attorneys on my team was unconsciously triggered. The wife was enraged at her husband's indulgences and poor money management during the marriage. Because he was the main wage earner, the husband felt he was entitled to use any and all of their remaining funds to continue his lifestyle.

The wife and her attorney bonded instantly as the "narcissistic husband" attempted to control the divorce process. The husband, used to being in total control of the marital finances, now had a new adversary, his wife's attorney, who "was not going to be bullied." The power struggle that ensued between the wife's attorney and the husband took on a life of its own. The case finally resolved after the husband fired his attorney and I, as the MHP, mediated the settlement between the husband and the wife's attorney.

On occasion, parallel process can have a strong positive effect on collaborative interactions. Modeling a team working effectively and respectfully can have a calming influence on emotional clients, one that encourages the clients toward a genuine attitude of collaboration. In these cases, it is not unusual for the divorcing couple to gain awareness that the team has facilitated the ending their marriage with respect and dignity. The clients have learned new interpersonal skills so they may effectively co-parent their children together afterward.

## CONTROL

Another reason why collaborative professionals struggle to retain their newly acquired behavior patterns relates to the fact that acting collaboratively necessarily requires some "loss of control." Each professional has long operated independently in her own domain and each is used to being "in charge" of the process. Collaborative process involves working as a team and teamwork means relinquishing some control to peers. This loss of control can bring about resistance and can create a sense of impotence. The lawyer may focus on particular behaviors of team members to confirm her fear that her legal expertise is not valued.

Examples of non-collaborative behavior regarding control include:

- Attorneys who need to attend all meetings with a client, even when they meet with the neutrals;
- Attorneys who speak for a client;
- Attorneys who don't allow clients to discuss possible resolution;
- Attorneys who have difficulty complying with the client's needs or requests, especially when "it would never happen in court;" and
- Attorneys who need to direct the process.

The perception of loss of control may cause the lawyer to overcompensate with legal rules or standards and unconsciously sabotage the collaboration. Other team members may also fall into reactivity, which reinforces the narrative that it is the other professionals who are challenging the best outcome for the client.

## PERSONALITY TRAITS AND TEAM DYNAMICS

Personality traits are the enduring patterns of behavior, temperament, and emotions that are the distinguishing qualities or characteristics of an individual. In the collaborative process, we seek to blend attorneys, MHPs, and FPs into a team. Each member of the team has different personality traits, as well as significantly diverse training, experience, and ways of conceptualizing situations. Each professional views the divorce from a different perspective and contributes his expertise to help the couple move toward a mutually acceptable settlement. Awareness of the distinct personality features of the professionals can lead to better management of team dynamics.

Character traits common to attorneys are explored in a study that collected data in 2009-2010 from nearly 2,000 lawyers at four large law firms.[2] Attorneys scored high in leadership and social skills as authoritarian and less subordinate and preferred active rather than passive roles in situations. They were portrayed as less concerned about emotional issues and tended to be analytical and strategic in how they approached problem-solving. The study suggested that they are self-critical, temperamental, and task-oriented and that they "speak their minds." Because of these traits, they can be perceived as "cold, critical, and argumentative," and can seem weak in interpersonal sensitivity. Other conclusions suggest that lawyers are "easily excitable" and can "become tense and overly critical."

MHPs are perceived as empathetic, compassionate, supportive, non-judgmental, and non-confrontational. They are trained in the variability of human behavior, listening and communication skills, and observation and interpretation of non-verbal behaviors. They tend not to be authoritarian or have control issues and are reactive rather than proactive in their interactions. When charged with the role of facilitator, not all MHPs are comfortable fulfilling that leadership position, especially if it means competing with the attorneys for the leadership role.

Financial professionals tend to be organized, systematic, logical, and structured. They are detail-oriented, mathematically skilled, comfortable with numbers, and cautious. They tend to be focused on problem-solving and minimizing emotional influences. They value honesty and are ethically focused. Their view of settlement may not incorporate the emotional needs of the family.

Despite these differences, the collaborative process should ideally lead to the perfect union of legal, mental health, and financial professionals working together. The caveat, of course, is that not all personalities work well together. Each professional has his own "personality style" and mindset. Each individual has her own ego, problems, and biases. The expectation that this new team, whose members may not be familiar with each other, can meld together seamlessly into the newly formed group may be illusory.

Frank discussion of the structure, needs, and roles of each participant in a pre-team meeting is critical to the realization of effective teamwork. The ultimate success or failure of the collaboration may well depend upon it.

## EMOTIONS

The emotional status of the couple and their relationship with each other can also have a significant influence on the entire process. Any emotional discord can be either exacerbated or diffused by the actions, words, and deeds of any member of the team. Guidance given by the professionals in their private meetings can also inadvertently damage or heal the fragile working bond between a couple drawn to the hope of a non-combative divorce.

Examples that may escalate the conflict between the couple include:

- Attorney or team member's covert collusion with a client against the spouse regarding significant issues;
- Attorney or team member's covert corroboration in the vilification of the spouse;
- Endorsement that a client has the "right to be heard" in a team meeting despite the potential volatility of a remark;
- Forwarding emails marked "professionals only" to a client; and
- Forwarding or sending emails to a client that contains inflammatory information about a spouse or a team member.

Examples that can defuse the conflict between the couple include:

- Reframing an emotional conflict into a positive outcome;
- Responding calmly and rationally to a dispute;
- Avoiding jumping to a conclusion or judgment;
- Using "I messages" and "active listening;" and
- Developing options and solutions to resolve issues.

In a divorce process, in which emotions play a powerful role, the probability of emotions spinning out of control is significantly increased when the professionals react negatively or non-collaboratively. This occurrence needs to be immediately identified, addressed, and managed by the team through the debriefing process.

## TRUST AND TEAM DYNAMICS

Building a strong collaborative team depends on several important components. The most important element is the establishment of trust and mutual respect between the team members. The cornerstones of the collaborative process— commitment to the process, honesty, respect, and transparency— depend on this trust. All members agree to share information openly and freely and to not fall back into traditional positional tactics. The team shares the goal of deeper resolution so members must establish clear roles and responsibilities to best support the clients. There needs to be accountability for the actions of each professional and an opportunity to discuss and resolve internal disputes. Building trust requires time and vulnerability, especially when starting a new collaborative matter with new colleagues. Trust is easily broken and difficult to repair. Staying focused on the goal of helping clients can help the team achieve its best result in a civil and respectful manner.

## TRUE POTENTIAL

Since January 2014, the Florida Academy of Collaborative Professionals, in conjunction with the International Academy of Collaborative Professionals, has been collecting data on collaborative family law cases in Florida. In preliminary findings, 49 surveys submitted through December 2015 identified several factors that were determined to cause a collaborative case to be considered "difficult" or cause the case to terminate. Factors included "lack of trust between the professionals, lack of teamwork, and different approaches or styles of advocacy." Despite some of the difficulties, 84% of collaborative cases reached conclusion with a full settlement agreement.

Given that any one of a multitude of factors can derail a collaborative matter, what can be done to prevent a case from unraveling? Can the mere knowledge and understanding of "why" dedicated collaborative professionals are not always able to remain "collaborative" be the solution? Or is there a more deliberate structure that needs to be imposed on the team? What can be done to prevent collaborative professionals from acting non-collaboratively? What can be done to avoid a team member acting like a "wolf in sheep's clothing?"

## WHAT THE PROFESSIONALS CAN DO
## BEFORE A COLLABORATIVE MATTER BEGINS

When your collaborative team is assembled, it is important to recommend to clients professionals who have a high likelihood of compatibility, who not only have been trained in the collaborative process but who have an awareness of the shift in perspective needed to do this work well. It is essential to have a pre-process team meeting of the professionals before the case begins, even if it is not billed to the clients. This informal meeting can establish a framework within which the team can operate in an effective mode. It can be a friendly introduction for new members to meet each other and can open the conversation for future management of inter/intra team dynamics.

The following checklists can provide suggestions when forming a collaborative team.

First, choose your collaborative teammates carefully.

- Choose professionals who have been trained in the collaborative process.
- Choose professionals who can check adversarial behaviors at the door.
- Choose professionals who are able to make the paradigm shift.
- Choose members who demonstrate respect for the other professionals.
- Choose professionals who can guide the clients through the collaborative process.
- Choose professionals who are able to attend and participate

81

in pre- and post-team meetings and debriefs.
- When a good team is assembled, stick with that team.
- Know your own buttons.
- Know your limitations.
- Identify "red flags."

Second, have a pre-process meeting and discuss the following:

- The role, expectations, and experience of each team member;
- How professional fee disparities will be handled;
- How pre-team meetings will be conducted;
- How team meetings will be conducted, including:
  - Where the meetings will occur;
  - Who will write and distribute the agenda;
  - Who will take minutes;
  - How the minutes will be distributed; and
  - When the clients will receive the minutes;
- How emails will be handled, including:
  - Who will get them;
  - Whether emails will be designated as "For Professionals Only;" and
  - Whether they will be shared with the clients, and, if so, when;
- How information sharing will be conducted;
- How often debriefings will occur;
- How debriefings will be conducted;
- How each professional will receive feedback/critique from other team members;
- Where and when each team member prefers to receive feedback; and
- How the team will handle and resolve intra-team conflicts.

Screen clients to determine if they have the capacity for the collaborative work. Clients being considered for collaborative divorce should be evaluated as to whether they demonstrate:

- Reasonable expectations;
- Willingness to listen to the other spouse;
- Willingness to participate;
- Willingness to be honest;
- Preferences for privacy;
- Willingness to reach a reach a fair, not a one-sided, settlement;
- Personal motivation;
- Ability to cooperate respectfully;
- Ability to share all relevant information;
- Ability to acknowledge fault;
- Ability to take responsibility for their own choices;
- Willingness to pass up their "day in court;"
- Comfort in working with the other spouse in the same room;
- Willingness to disclose sensitive information; and
- Willingness to work with and not against the other spouse for mutually acceptable results.

Other considerations include:
- A power imbalance between the spouses;
- A history of domestic violence; and
- Whether the client continues to insist that the divorce proceed in an adversarial manner.

## WHAT IF YOU ARE COLLABORATING WITH A "WOLF IN SHEEP'S CLOTHING"?

Despite extensive precautions, there may well come a time when one of the professionals reverts to non-collaborative behavior. The following suggestions may be helpful when confronted by the proverbial "wolf in sheep's clothing":

- Give authentic, non-critical feedback to the "wolf;"
- Give objective, concrete examples of the non-collaborative interaction;
- Ask for help from the MHP to address what you may be doing to provoke the non-collaborative attitude;

- Use the team debrief to address the problem with the other professional in a safe setting; and
- Debrief! Debrief! Debrief!

The effectiveness of a team debrief rests strongly on the creation of a supportive, learning environment of trust and safety. It needs to be a safe place to express feelings and encourage authentic feedback and communication. The debrief should occur immediately after the team meeting or soon thereafter. It should begin with some type of positive reinforcement, a review of the goals of the meeting, and a discussion about what happened. Each professional should be given the opportunity to explore and deal with the feelings experienced during the collaborative meeting. There should be direction provided by the MHP for improvement and acknowledgement that mistakes are a part of the learning process. The debrief should not be used as a platform for criticism, blame, or finger-pointing.

Another resource is the collaborative practice group. The team at impasse may discuss the issue with an objective, experienced, collaboratively trained colleague who will preserve confidentiality of the case. Utilize that person in any of the following ways:

- As a consultant to defuse non-collaborative behavior;
- To work in conjunction with the MHP;
- As a neutral mediator to help settle the case; and/or
- As a mentor to the "wolf."

## CONCLUSION

The intent of this chapter is to raise the awareness of collaborative professionals regarding non-collaborative behavior. The "paradigm shift," described so casually as an easy "conversion," is actually a very complex and difficult transition to make and sustain. It is hoped that, by understanding the interaction and confluence of many factors that impact the emotionally charged environment of a divorce for both the clients and their professionals, the team itself can correct and redirect these non-collaborative lapses.

The collaborative process truly offers the public the best chance of saving familial relationships after a divorce. In spite of growing pains and occasional "slips," the collaborative model is still, by far, the best method by which to divorce. By utilizing the power of a well-trained, carefully selected team, instances of non-collaborative behavior can be minimized and eventually overcome.[3]

---

[1] This chapter was printed in the Spring 2017 edition of the *Collaborative Review*, which gave permission to reprint it in this anthology.

[2] Richard, Larry Dr., "Herding Cats: The Lawyer Personality Revealed," LAWPRO Magazine "Personality & Practice," Winter 2008 (Vol. 7 no. 1).

[3] Anderson, M. "The role of group personality composition in the emergence of task and relationship conflict within groups." *Journal of Management and Organization* 15.1 (2009): 82-96. ABI/INFORM Global, ProQuest. Web. 1 Dec. 2010. *Handbook of Advances in Trust Research,* edited by Bachmann, R. and Zaheer, A., Chapter 2. The role of trust in negotiation processes, Roy J. Lewicki and Beth Polin, 2012, pp. 29–54.

Lana M. Stern, Ph.D., is a licensed psychologist, marriage and family therapist, parent coordinator, and Florida Supreme Court certified mediator. Dr. Stern has been in private practice in the Coral Gables, Florida, area for the past 30 years.

She is a member of the American, Florida, and Dade County Psychological Associations, the International and Florida Associations of Family and Conciliation Courts, and the International Academy of Collaborative Professionals.

Dr. Stern serves on the IACP trainers network and development committee. She is an active member of the Collaborative Family Law Institute of Miami. She is a past vice president and currently serves on the CFLI board and the membership, education, and mentoring committees. She is a member of the Florida Academy of Collaborative Professionals, serving as a board member, delegate, chair of the training and webinar committees, and co-chair of the annual collaborative conference.

Dr. Stern has lectured extensively on the role of the neutral mental health professional in the collaborative law process. She was an adjunct professor at Florida International University for six years, supervising master's level mental health and school counselors during their practicum and internship. She co-taught the first collaborative law workshop at the University of Miami School of Law in the spring of 2012.

Dr. Stern has presented multiple basic and advanced trainings to attorneys, mental health professionals, and financial professionals in Miami, Tampa, Gainesville, Boca Raton, Jacksonville, and Panama City, Florida, as well as in New Hampshire. She has worked extensively in collaborative family law cases as the mental health professional/facilitator. She co-authored the chapter on collaborative law in The Florida Bar CLE book, *Dissolution of Marriage*. Dr. Stern co-founded Florida Collaborative Trainers, an interdisciplinary training group. She presented at the IACP forum in Texas in 2013 and again in Vancouver, BC, in 2014.

Dr. Stern can be reached at lmsternphd@aol.com, www.drlanamstern.com, and www.floridacollaborativetrainers.com.

*Mental health professionals new to collaborative practice may find themselves in a catch-22: they want to gain collaborative experience, but other collaborative professionals won't ask them to be on their teams because they do not have experience yet. It may feel like they have to just sit and wait for an attorney to take a chance on them and include them on a team.*

*And the more time that goes by without working on a collaborative matter after being trained, the more likely it is that the collaborative skills the professional learned at training will be forgotten. Relationships the professional formed during training may evaporate. The feeling that the professional experienced at training that collaborative is a better way may begin to fade.*

*So what is a mental health professional to do? Is it possible to market oneself in a manner that promotes inclusion on collaborative teams? Is there a way for the mental health professional to bring cases to himself? After all, the more teams on which you participate, the more collaborative relationships you will form, the more experience you will gain, and the more likely you will be included on future teams.*

## BACKDOOR COLLABORATIVE
### BY GARY DIRENFELD, MSW, RSW

Collaborative practice offers clients different models so that they can choose the one that best fits their needs. The first model is the basic team model consisting of two lawyers and two clients. Beyond that is an expanded team model that includes a mental health professional who may play a variety of roles, as well as a financial professional. If need be, other ancillary professionals can be brought to the team, such as a business valuator or perhaps a realtor.

There are two schools of thought about deployment of the expanded team. The first is on an "as need" basis, as determined by the lawyers. The other is referred to as a "full team model" where everyone is on board from the get-go.

Regardless of approach, though, collaborative practice is a lawyer-centric practice. It is the family lawyer who is in control of the model deployed and who gets chosen to play on the team. Like kids organizing themselves in the schoolyard to play a game of baseball, two lawyers acting as captains pick members of their team from the pool of available professionals. Showing their fancy bat or glove, the allied professionals wait at the side hopefully displaying the right stuff in order to be picked for the team.

What neither the lawyers nor most of the other professionals realize is that there is another model of practice that is not lawyer-centric, which does not depend on the predilection of the lawyer to determine the team. I call this "backdoor collaborative." In this bottom-up model of practice, other professionals do not have to wait to be invited to the dance by the lawyer. The other professionals can directly market their practice to separating couples and serve as the entry point to a collaboratively informed separation process. Even if referred to by litigating attorneys to mediate a parenting plan, the mental health professional or financial professional can still turn the file into a *collaboratively informed* process.

One approach to the backdoor model of collaborative practice is to market services to family doctors for marriages on the cusp. Family doctors are the front line for persons presenting with depression and anxiety, which are key symptoms of stress that are often related to a troubled relationship. While the physician may offer a medicinal intervention, if they so much as scratch the surface for social contributors to the depression or anxiety, they may find a troubled relationship beneath. In such circumstances, informed physicians know they can send their patient to a mental health practitioner who works at the intersection of mental health, troubled relationships, and family law matters.

When their patient calls and has a couple-related relationship issue, both persons are invited to attend to address the relationship. Depending on their goals and the state of the relationship, some relationships are improved and some couples are aided in separating. Assuming separation, the couple can be helped to develop a parenting plan. They can also be referred to a financial professional as may be necessary for the determination of the distribution of assets, spousal support, and child support. Addressing the relationship issues, regardless of direction, helps to abate depression and anxiety by bringing structure to the issues at hand.

When the parenting plan and financial plan have been determined, then the separating couple can be referred to collaboratively trained lawyers to do what lawyers really do best, craft contracts. In this way, the values of collaborative practice are maintained—two separating persons maintaining control of process options for their separation as well as maintaining control of the outcome. The value of referring to collaboratively trained lawyers after the parenting plan and financial matters have been sorted out is to reduce the likelihood of client agreements being opened up by litigiously oriented lawyers with the promise of "I can getcha more."

In circumstances where separating parents are referred by litigation lawyers to help develop a parenting plan, it is not uncommon to learn that there are unsettled financial issues waiting to be sorted out too. Given the rapport developed with the parents through mediating the parenting plan, the mediator may offer to facilitate a five-way meeting to help address their financial issues. These offers are almost always acted upon as it is both parents who are driving this home to their lawyers. The parents have assumed control of the process and are setting the expectations for the lawyers to follow suit.

## CASE EXAMPLE: CHARLENE AND RICK

Charlene was referred by her family doctor for counseling. At telephone intake, Charlene spoke of being sad and overwhelmed by matters originating with her marriage. She discovered that her husband of seven years, Rick, was now involved in his second affair. Upon confronting him, Rick told her he would do anything to save the marriage, including attending counseling. The counselor saw the couple within a week. However, while Rick wanted to maintain the marriage, Charlene did not. They had two young children, and her concern was how to manage their care between them as separated parents.

Rick was remorseful and didn't want to pressure Charlene about her decision. He had his own wounds to lick in consideration of his behavior and realized he needed to concentrate on his life with the children going forward.

Together Charlene and Rick sorted out a parenting plan that respected their roles and work schedules. They determined a plan for their physical separation and knew that it hinged partially upon sorting out the value of their home and determining mutual financial obligations. They were referred to a divorce financial professional to aid them in sorting those issues.

After they figured out solutions to their financial issues, they returned to put some fine details on the parenting plan and to develop a script to share with their kids: the story of their situation and separation and what was to come. They also determined the narrative they would share with friends and extended kin, knowing that they didn't want any negative influences to come back upon the children through any third party.

With everything sorted out, they were then referred to individual collaborative lawyers to formalize their agreements, both financial and parental. With the agreement formalized, they implemented their plans and carried on.

While on the one hand, this case example appears to be of a low conflict couple, it should be noted that it has elements that, if managed differently, could have been turned into a high-conflict case. Charlene's anger about Rick's second affair could have been exploited. She could have been positioned to act out her anger through the children and/or the division of assets to expunge her upset, if not humiliation, for being cheated on twice. How these matters enter third party processes to address distress has much to do with the outcome. In this case, the couple entered through a clinical process where the aim is to reduce stress and conflict regardless of whether remaining intact as a couple or separating, as per the couple's goals.

## CASE EXAMPLE: SANJAY AND MEENA

Sanjay and Meena separated about a year prior to referral. They each had their own lawyer, neither of whom had collaborative training. Both Sanjay and Meena were living with their respective parents. They had two elementary school-aged children. Their house sat empty, and they were in dispute over the parenting plan. They already had high legal bills and were of limited means. They were referred for mediation to resolve the parenting plan.

Sanjay had initiated the separation, unsatisfied with married life. Meena felt betrayed although there was no other woman in the picture and this was not a matter of dispute. She felt he didn't deserve to see the children and acted as gatekeeper. She hinted at domestic violence, but there was no tangible evidence to support what were really only insinuations. Indeed, she appeared to yield more control of Sanjay and the situation than he of anything. Sanjay was only hoping for a regular schedule of parenting time. He was concerned that his business would be overvalued and that this would undermine his livelihood. The parents were in dispute about the value of his business, as well as the quantum and duration of spousal and child support.

In mediation, Sanjay and Meena agreed that the mediator would meet with the children to hear their stories and concerns and would bring their voices to the process. It was clear that while aligned with their mother, they did miss their father and sought to see him regularly as long as it didn't upset their mother.

Meena and Sanjay reached a tentative parenting agreement, subject to the determination of financial matters. The issues were being connected as bargaining chips to assure satisfaction in both areas before reaching an overall agreement. Both clients came to trust the mediator and viewed the mediator as neutral. Realizing that they would not settle on the parenting matters in the absence of settling the financial matters, the mediator offered to facilitate a five-way meeting to get the financial settlement process on track.

Meena and Sanjay agreed to ask their lawyers to convene a meeting, facilitated by the mediator. Both lawyers called the mediator to question the necessity of the meeting. It was explained how well the parents did in achieving a tentative parenting plan but that it remained fragile, subject to the settlement of financial matters. The professionals and clients agreed to a five-way meeting. Therein, with some suggestions put forth by the mediator, the clients agreed to a single business valuator to assess the business and report back at another five-way meeting. Other financial documents were to also be in place for the meeting. The process was delicate and took several meetings throughout which were the ongoing threats of litigation. The mediator as facilitator helped all persons maintain the process, and finally, the clients achieved an overall settlement.

This process was never referred to by the mediator as collaborative as it did not seem that would be tolerated by the attorneys. However, this was very much a collaboratively informed process, which in turn kept the matter from unraveling or going to litigation.

If we think rigidly about collaborative practice requiring a set process or type of team to facilitate a separation process and outcome, the movement will be limited in scope and breadth. In my view, collaborative practice is more about an attitude, a way of thinking about how we help separated couples transition to new models of relationships. Backdoor collaborative is just a way of conceptualizing more flexible thinking about how we can help couples transition. At heart are several key values, including self-determination, the client remaining in control of the process and the outcome, and respectful service and conciliatory approaches with creative problem-solving.

Gary Direnfeld, MSW, RSW, is a social worker. Courts in Ontario, Canada, consider him an expert in social work, marital and family therapy, child development, parent-child relations, and custody and access matters. Mr. Direnfeld is the host of the TV reality show *Newlywed/Nearly Dead*, a parenting columnist for *The Hamilton Spectator*, and the author of *Marriage Rescue: Overcoming the Ten Deadly Sins in Failing Relationships*.

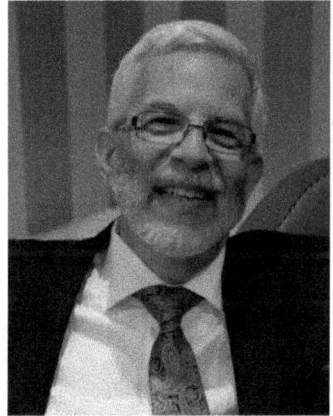

He is a sought-after speaker on matters of family life as well as building successful peacemaking practices. With more than 400 radio, television, and print interviews to his credit, he is also highly sought for his opinion on matters concerning parenting and social issues. His popular website www.yoursocialworker.com contains a library of his more than 300 articles and serves as an open and free resource for parents and other professionals.

Mr. Direnfeld maintains a private practice in Dundas and Georgina, Ontario, providing a range of services for people in distress. He speaks at conferences and workshops throughout North America and was the first social worker to sit on the Ontario Board for Collaborative Family Law.

*In a two-coach collaborative model, the mental health professional takes on different roles than he would in a one-coach model. Whereas in the one-coach model, the mental health professional acts as a neutral, in the two-coach model, each client has his own coach who works as an advocate for his rights.*

*Whether a one-coach model or two-coach model is utilized typically depends on the norm of the specific community. However, just because a certain model is regularly utilized in your community does not mean that the other model should not be adapted based on the needs of the specific couple. Two-coach models can be especially useful in matters where there are power imbalances, domestic violence, addictions, and mental health issues. In these sensitive matters, the clients may feel more comfortable if they each have their own advocate.*

*Opponents of the two-coach model argue that it can make the matter more adversarial, more "us against them." Further, adding yet another professional to the team can make the process more expensive and less attractive to the average family in conflict. It can make meetings even more difficult to schedule, thus causing the matter to take longer to resolve. But proponents point out that if a two-coach model results in better, fairer resolutions, then it is worth the additional cost and time.*

## THE ART OF CO-COACHING
### BY PATRICE COURTEAU MA, LMFT AND
### MARVIN CHAPMAN, PSY.D., LMFT, CFC

Divorce is a major life transition. While it marks the end of one part of the client's life, it is also the beginning of another. Collaborative divorce coaches help the clients manage the pain and strain of restructuring relationships while focusing on goals for the present and the future. Working with the client to make the most of their strengths, the collaborative divorce coaches assist the clients in being their best during the divorce process while taking positive steps toward a new independent life.

For the professionals working in the collaborative divorce arena, the pleasure of working with like-minded individuals who see the value in helping clients work peacefully through their divorce process is a gift. Two collaborative divorce coaches working in synchronicity with each other for the benefit of their clients is often an art form in itself.

The following is an example of synchronicity from a recent case.

Sarah and James had been married for 27 years. Sarah was a kind and pleasant woman with a somber appearance. James was a reserved man with a warm smile. They had come to a point when they realized that their attempts at couple's therapy were fruitless. Along the way, they had lost the desire to work on the communication in their marriage. Each had felt the profound sadness of their long-term marriage coming to an end. They had raised children together, taken care of their family home, and worked hard in their traditional roles to raise their family. Sarah had been a stay-at-home mom, and James had worked hard to financially support the family.

The couple's therapist shared a website called Collaborative Divorce Solutions of Orange County (www.cdsoc.com) with them and urged them to consider a collaborative divorce.

Although their children were grown, Sarah and James each had a strong desire to maintain a positive relationship with one another so they could both attend family gatherings and events they didn't want to miss in the future. They understood that this likely would not happen if they chose an adversarial divorce process.

Sarah shared with her coach, Patrice:

> When interviewing a litigation attorney, I had sensed a "we will go after everything you are entitled to" attitude that didn't sit well with me. I'm not in love with James any longer, but I don't want to enter into a battle. I have seen the effects

of the battle on friends, in their divorces, and I don't want this for my family.

James shared a similar thought with his coach, Marv:

> I have seen too many of my friends' families be destroyed during the litigation process. Now, they can't be in the same place together, which ruins all of their adult children's special events. It is a shame.

At their first four-way meeting, which included the clients and their coaches, they worked together to create their Statement of Highest Intentions:

> It is our goal through this process to create an amicable agreement, sharing family resources in a way that we can both be comfortable as we move forward. It is also our goal to create a friendly atmosphere for our children and their children at family gatherings as we move into our independent lives.

After they created their Statement of Highest Intentions, Marv and Patrice helped James and Sarah continue to build on the communication skills they both had been working on individually with their coaches. Both James and Sarah had had the opportunity to share what was most difficult for them when communicating with each other.

They reached a point in this four-way meeting where Patrice and Marv felt that Sarah and James would benefit most from seeing a way to process and share information differently than they had in their married life. That moment when you know your professional counterpart is on the same page you are and is willing to trust your instinct and their own to role-play for clients how they could communicate differently is an example of synchronicity. Without missing a beat, Marv and Patrice looked at each other. Marv said to Sarah and James, "Give us just a moment. We are going to talk as if you are not sitting here in the room with us."

Patrice said, "I have a question."

Marv replied, "I think I am thinking the same thing."

What both were thinking and Patrice said aloud was, "What if they each knew how much they individually appreciated the other's part in raising their family?"

Marv and Patrice turned to James and Sarah and noticed a shift in their body language. Sarah hung her head subtly, and James looked down at the floor. Sarah softly shared, "I am only a housewife."

James seemed at a loss to reply. Marv with his experience, wisdom, and timing, something so appreciated when working with client-centered professionals, softly stated, "You are so much more than a housewife," while looking at Sarah.

Patrice softly shared, looking at James, "And you are so much more than a wage earner."

Because Patrice and Marv trusted the intimacy of co-coaching, they allowed the stillness and the tears in the room to linger. What they had just done was to allow Sarah and James to feel the intimacy of a co-coaching and the shift that can come from the synchronicity between collaborative colleagues when they are helping clients create a shift in themselves.

After a few moments had passed, James looked at Sarah and said, "I appreciate all the time and effort you have given to raising our children."

Sarah, looking at James replied, "I appreciate all your hard work and how much you have been able to provide for our family while allowing me to stay at home with our children all those years."

That shift we felt as professionals, and more importantly that Sarah and James experienced, is the essence of the work in collaborative divorce coaching.

Communication between the co-coaches requires confidence, compatibility of coaching styles, congruency, safety, like-minded appreciation of empathy for clients, faith in the process, and trust in your collaborative colleague. Communication is the key to successful outcomes of collaborative divorce coaching. To visualize how the synchronicity works is to imagine a figure eight, a continuous loop that creates a safe environment for the clients to feel heard and understood and for the co-coaches to mirror, reflect back, and provide feedback to their clients. It is the collaborative divorce coaches who assist the clients in finding a better way to communicate. Often, this is helped by the clients imitating what they see and hear their coaches doing in one-on-one coaching sessions and in their four-way meetings.

Each and every case helps coaches hone their skills. Advanced trainings are a blessing. Training other professionals in this field also helps create even more trust between collaborative coaches on a collaborative team. The most important aspect of this work is to remember what an honor and a privilege it is to work with clients going through one of the most difficult experiences in their lives.

Once Sarah and James had the opportunity to shift into a better way to process and share information, they were able to move from the emotional quicksand in which couples often find themselves caught. They were better able to begin Agreement Readiness work of creating Options for Resolutions in the collaborative divorce process. Again, divorce is a major life transition. The skills that Sarah and James were learning and incorporating into their daily lives and interactions had a positive effect on their divorce process.

Giving clients every opportunity to live their Statement of Highest Intentions profoundly affects their children, extended families, friends, neighbors, and community long after the divorce is complete. By taking the shame or blame out of the divorce process while managing the pain associated with divorce, clients are more likely to create better relationships and healthier futures.

Finally, the gift of working with like-minded collaborative professionals not only has a powerful effect post-divorce for the couple and their family but also on the professionals. Collaborative professionals talk often about the benefits they experience by working in this field. They are constantly challenged and typically work longer hours than in their private practices. Yet the teamwork and the synergy created by working with professionals you admire and learn from daily make this work dynamic and life changing.

Having experienced divorce herself, Patrice Courteau MA, LMFT, is committed to helping couples and families find a peaceful way to uncouple and still maintain the wellbeing of their family. She is passionate about helping individuals find the balance and direction to move forward, grow from the divorce experience, and ultimately find the joy that may have been missing from their lives.

Ms. Courteau is a licensed mental health professional, psychotherapist, divorce coach, and child specialist. She has served as a board member of Collaborative Divorce Solutions of Orange County and currently serves as vice president. She is a member of Collaborative Practice of California (CP Cal), International Association of Collaborative Professionals, Collaborative Divorce Education Institute, California Association of Marriage and Family Therapists, and a past member of American Association of Marriage and Family Therapists. She is a certified instructor for the High Conflict Diversion Program, volunteer mediator for the Orange County Court, and past member of Woody Mosten's study group.

Ms. Courteau's background includes mediation training, full team interdisciplinary collaborative divorce training, shadow training for the Train the Trainer Program, and advanced interdisciplinary collaborative training. She has presented at CP Cal and is currently a trainer for the Collaborative Divorce Education Institute. She has also been trained and received advanced training in the one-coach model. Ms. Courteau is a credentialed K-12 teacher and volunteers countless hours for the Divorce Recovery Program at St. Andrews Church in Newport Beach.

Ms. Courteau has a passion for public speaking and has been asked to present numerous times on various topics related to peacemaking in divorce and divorce recovery. She has been interviewed on radio stations and has contributed to publications on divorce.

If you are interested in learning more and would like to reach

Ms. Courteau directly, she can be reached at 1151 Dove Street, Suite 280, Newport Beach, CA, 92660, 949-525-7375, patricecourteau@yahoo.com.

Marvin L. Chapman Psy.D., LMFT, CFC, has been divorce coaching for over 30 years, commencing when he co-founded a nonprofit organization emphasizing responsible fatherhood. He is currently the president of this multiple award-winning nonprofit organization. Dr. Chapman learned that empowering individuals with information about family court and the effect it has on family members significantly reduces the anxiety, frustration, and confusion inherently present when entering the family court system.

In the early 1980s, Dr. Chapman was fortunate to be mentored by some of the innovative pioneers of court-mandated mediation, Hugh McIsaac and Ron Hulbert. Dr. Chapman is a strong advocate for out-of-court options and non-adversarial alternatives, a product of his witnessing firsthand the pervasive abusiveness of the adversarial family court process on individuals and families.

In 1986, Dr. Chapman was appointed to the California Senate Task Force on Family Equity, a task force set up by the California legislature to make recommendations relating to family law. He was appointed to this task force to represent the issues and concerns confronting fathers in family court.

Through the following decades, Dr. Chapman spread the word through public speaking, writing articles, and serving on the board of directors for *Modern Dad* magazine and as board member and professional standards chairperson with the California Association of Legal Document Assistants.

In 2001, the Orange County District Attorney Family Support Division selected Dr. Chapman to present *The Father's Perspective* for their customer service training.

Dr. Chapman's work with fathers was recognized in 2001, 2002, and 2004 by receipt of community service awards from Disneyland Resort. The 2004 award was the prestigious *Jack B. Lindquist Award*, the highest recognition bestowed by Disneyland

Resort. The 2004 award was presented the last year in which Disneyland Resort recognized nonprofit organizations through their community service award program.

Dr. Chapman earned a Bachelor of Arts in psychology, a Master of Science in counseling, and a doctorate in psychology, with a forensic psychology specialty. In 2004, he took training to become a collaborative divorce coach and has become an active member of several collaborative divorce practice groups in Southern California. In 2010, Dr. Chapman became a collaborative divorce trainer.

Education and training have given Dr. Chapman the tools—and working with families for over three decades has given him the experience—to effectively guide and assist those going through the family reorganization process. His approach is information, education, and communication. He is solution orientated, empowering individuals with conflict resolution skills. He assists individuals in identifying and defusing hot emotional issues and recognizing behavioral roadblocks that interfere with making healthy decisions. Dr. Chapman actively seeks viable options, constructive alternatives, and positive solutions for all family members.

If you are interested in learning more and would like to reach Mr. Chapman directly, he can be reached at 714-329-3532, divorcecoachmarvinchapman@gmail.com.

*Many mental health professionals appreciate the two-coach collaborative model because they are able to work closely with another mental health practitioner with a common goal of helping a family to create an agreement that meets their most important goals and interests. The coaches work with each of their clients to help them understand the other spouse's perspective and how this information can be helpful in coming to the most optimum agreement possible.*

*When a two-coach model is used, it is especially important to ensure that the team does not become adversarial. A natural hostility may arise when each client has his own attorney and his own coach all sitting together on one side of the table during a highly stressful and emotional time, seemingly facing off against the other side, with a financial neutral in the middle. The coaches must work together to focus the team toward the clients' common goals and to point out the similarities in their desires, i.e. to maintain strong relationships with the children, to reach a fair distribution of assets and liabilities, to be able to live comfortably based on the amount of support paid and received, etc.*

*When coaches work well together in the two-coach model, collaborative magic happens.*

## THE EVOLUTION OF THE DIVORCE STORY:
### THE COACHES' VERSION
### BY PEGGY THOMPSON, PH.D. AND NANCY J. ROSS LCSW, BCD

*Through the eyes of Elizabeth and Sandy, two clients going through divorce, Peggy Thompson and Nancy Ross discuss their roles as co-coaches in the collaborative divorce process in helping their clients co-create a new post-divorce story that realizes their hopes of a healthier, more connected relationship.*

## STORIES: WHAT THEY ARE AND THE ROLE THEY PLAY IN OUR LIVES

What is it about stories? They define us. They help us make sense of our world and our relationships. We use them to find personal direction, to explain our actions, and even to provide meaning in our lives. Yet, so often, our personal stories remain both unexamined and unshared.

Embedded in our family of origin, shaped in part by our family's values—and often in opposition to those same values—we create our personal story of who we are and how we relate to our world. One may consider himself a person of integrity; or one who has to fight the injustices of the world; or one who is a self-made, "can do" individual; or perhaps one who values serving others; or even one who believes he needs to control others and thus avoid being controlled in return. Our stories are endlessly complex and often not clearly thought out or fully developed, even as we separate from our family of origin and enter into relationships with others who have their own personal stories.

When two individuals marry, they face the inevitable challenge of defining themselves as individuals, of honoring their own stories while creating a new story together that, at least in a healthy marriage, allows for both personal and relationship growth. When it doesn't work, when neither individual feels loved and accepted by the other, when their stories don't mesh, the road toward divorce is paved as their stories become increasingly narrow and negative.

## CREATING THE STORY OF DIVORCE
### OR "WHY CAN'T I BE ME AND BE LOVED AND RESPECTED BY YOU?"

So it was for our clients, Elizabeth and Sandy.

Elizabeth was a prim-looking woman in her fifties who always wore pearls that trimmed her plump face. She first contacted a collaborative lawyer when Sandy informed her that he could no longer be married to her. Coming from a family of some wealth, she wished to maintain her family's privacy and achieve a "civilized" divorce while protecting her adult children from further damage.

Her lawyer, upon hearing her story of anger and betrayal, suggested she talk to Peggy.

In the meantime, Sandy's lawyer suggested Nancy as his coach. Initially, Sandy was resistant to the idea of a coach. He was a fierce business professional and didn't consider himself the type to need the help of someone whom he considered to be a therapist. Somewhat reluctantly, he met with Nancy. He was a balding man who typically wore grey pinstriped suits over brightly colored collared shirts and ties. He seemed to have a different expensive watch for each day of the week. And his shoes were always polished to a shine (almost as shiny as his balding head!).

Peggy soon learned that Elizabeth's view of their divorce was one of complete betrayal. She described to Peggy how her family helped each other out, both financially and emotionally. She prided herself on bringing those same values to her marriage, helping Sandy out whenever he needed her, raising their three children in his absence, even sharing "her" money with him when he wanted to indulge in his hobby as a collector of high-end bicycles and racing sailboats. While she expressed her love and respect for Sandy, she was also extremely angry with him because she felt he didn't participate in marriage counseling and had chosen to quit the marriage instead.

All this fueled her anger, creating a vengeful attitude that covered up her pain. This was then translated in her declaration to her lawyer:

> I want everything the law says I'm owed. I've devoted my life to him, and he's shut me out of it. He owes me a lot, including all the money I gave him that he spent on his ridiculous hobby. I want a tough negotiator on my side.

> I just don't trust him. He's a powerful man, and that scares me. He's more than a bully. He puts me down and makes it seem as if I'm stupid. He doesn't value who I am or anything I do. He only sees the world his way.

In Sandy's first meeting with Nancy, he described himself as a "self-made venture capitalist:"

> I made my way in life the hard way, something Elizabeth would never understand. I don't want a divorce, but it's the only way I can breathe. I can't be who she wants me to be. She wants a homebody who is predictable, and that's not me. We haven't been intimate in years. She's a good woman who constantly subjects herself to other's needs. I don't know who she is anymore, but I don't feel any attraction toward her. I love her as I might a sister, but, as I'm growing older, I don't want my marriage to be like that.
>
> I like adventure. I'm intellectually curious. I welcome challenges. Elizabeth can't understand that. She's satisfied with being the family nurturer. She's growing old before my eyes with her ideas of service and sacrifice. That's just not who I am. There's no passion in our relationship, and, at my core, I'm a passionate man. I'm afraid of losing that passion if I stay with her. I know that sounds selfish. I'm hurting my whole family and I'm scared of the future, I just don't have any other answer.

### PUTTING THE STORIES TOGETHER: THE COACH'S ROLE

Our role is to "join"' each of our clients in appreciating and accepting his or her story, while at the same time, helping each other "pull out" of the hypnotic trance of our client's view of reality to create a deeper understanding of the other client. Our co-coach offers an invitation to an alternative—the other client's story. That means we have to give up on the rightness or wrongness of our attachment to our client's story. When we can truly accept this invitation, we've discovered that we can open endless possibilities in the creation of a new, more productive story that will define the clients' new relationship in ways their divorce story could not. No other process of divorce offers this or attempts to achieve this vision.

Achieving this vision, as it turns out, is not easy. Divorce itself comes to us embedded in our cultural experience of an adversarial process. One person is right and the other is, by definition, wrong. One will win (meaning that his story prevails), and the other will lose. All of us as team members, not just coaches, are impacted and drawn into the client's conflict with this history. Hearing our client's story, we see it only from his eyes: a victim or an abuser; a leaver or a leavee. Justified or not, we can so easily get stuck in our client's story that we become the advocates of his divorce story rather than catalysts for a new understanding. Our job is to take these positional fragments and help the clients weave them into a more coherent, shared story—the "re-storying" of their relationship, not just their divorce story.

We didn't start out that way with Elizabeth and Sandy. Peggy and Elizabeth's lawyer initially identified with her story of sacrifice and abuse, while Nancy became immersed in Sandy's deep frustration and anger at losing his wife to her own ideals. We were able to support each of them in their story while creating a larger, more coherent story that helped them redefine their relationship going forward. We were successful, in part, due to the science and art of coaching, as well as because of the relationship that is created between the two coaches and each coach's relationship with her client.

Like most people, we wanted a reasonably simple explanation to why things had gone so wrong for this couple, thus the pull of the client's explanation. It was easy to believe that Sandy was experiencing a mid-life crisis that blinded him to the value of his partner or to see him as a dishonest, selfish egoist. It was equally easy to see Elizabeth as the wife who had turned herself into a self-sacrificing martyr who couldn't appreciate her husband. However, the more we shared, the less simple their relationship story became, allowing each of us to begin the crucial shift in embracing the more complex narrative of who they were and how that had impacted their relationship.

Each coach had an interesting view on Elizabeth and Sandy's relationship. According to Nancy:

I think I was able to allow Elizabeth's view into the mix because Peggy so clearly understood her and, rather than state Elizabeth's view as fact, she described the wholeness of her personality: her strengths, as well as her fears. This helped me relax, in that I didn't have to be the standard bearer for Sandy's point of view, explaining his actions and defending him to the other team members.

Instead, it opened up a new narrative, one that let me truly appreciate how the two of them came to this point in their lives. So much of this "coaches' dance" is embedded in the trust I have for Peggy and the keen insights she brings to her client and to the process itself. I think we modeled this understanding and acceptance for our clients together, using our shared knowledge to intervene and challenge their "divorce story" in a way they could accept.

Similarly, Peggy appreciated Nancy's contribution to the team:

I was able to hear Sandy's story from Nancy because I trust her as a clinician and because we have a history of working together. She also has the ability to explain her client in nonjudgmental terms rather than using diagnostic terms. She could describe what Sandy was really feeling and not the controlling image he was projecting. This helped me understand Sandy as an emotionally complex individual, not the one-dimensional person who Elizabeth saw. I began to see him through Nancy's eyes, while at the same time she was open to hearing me describe Elizabeth's feelings.

This sharing allowed us to mutually help our

clients shift from their divorce story and begin to create a new narrative together, built more on understanding their mutual intentions, and less on the rationalization of the divorce.

## IN THE ROOM: COACHES AND CLIENTS TOGETHER

The first meeting began painfully. As most individuals do at the beginning of their divorce, each began to lay out their divorce story, an explanation of how the other person had caused the problems in the marriage. Elizabeth noted how Sandy was condescending and dismissive of her as a wife and mother and how he didn't appreciate who she was or what she had done for their marriage. Sandy countered aggressively, "You killed our relationship a long time ago with your criticism and holier than thou attitude. You shut me out of your life and the children's as well." And so they began, each protecting himself/herself from the fear that the other might have some elements of truth in their accusation by reiterating their well-honed divorce story.

About ten minutes into the initial meeting, Peggy challenged Sandy as Elizabeth told her version of her divorce story, "Sandy, please don't interrupt Elizabeth's rendition of her story."

Sandy angrily turned to Elizabeth saying, "I don't need to hear this 'bad-guy' stuff again. This is getting us nowhere. I'm tired of being the 'bad guy' in our relationship, and you're always so perfect."

However, it was a turning point when Nancy looked at Sandy and said, "Sandy, let's sit back and see what Elizabeth has to say. Peggy can help with that, so it's not just the same 'bad guy story'. Let's listen." Nancy was "his" coach, and he felt she understood and accepted him. Because of that relationship, she had permission to challenge him in a way that no one else did.

In that moment, Elizabeth and Sandy might have drawn the coaches into siding with each of them, or the coaches could have found themselves bogged down in the pull of their negative justifications in a kind of righteous standoff. The couple would have repeated a version of the many conversations that they had developed so well in their marriage where Sandy shut down

Elizabeth's criticism with contemptuous anger, and she reacted to his disgust and eventual withdrawal by turning away and getting support from others. Peggy kept her from leaving the argument, helping her deepen it and begin to find the underlying fears that were driving her anger. It began to be easier for Sandy to hear her when it wasn't about his transgressions. The story became about her disappointing him, of not trusting herself to understand him, of feeling she had failed him. His became one of sadness and guilt that they really didn't "get" each other and how he felt he had failed her.

Sandy never challenged Peggy again. He did listen. Elizabeth, with Peggy's guidance, broadened her story to touch on common areas and values they shared, "We were friends at one time. We shared interests and goals. We had common interests."

Each valued the integrity of the other and expressed a sense of gratitude for what the other had brought to their marriage

Elizabeth expressed to Sandy, "I appreciate how hard you worked and your contributions to the marriage."

Sandy responded by becoming reflective, "I remember how you supported my work early on, and I appreciate how your family resources helped us lead the lifestyle we enjoyed."

Elizabeth tearfully replied, "I'm so sad that our marriage is ending."

With tears in his eyes, Sandy responded, "I'm so sorry that it has to be this way."

The story was beginning to shift; their anger and guilt no longer the driving force. Even the differences that had become a source of tension in their marriage were beginning to be acknowledged without the usual condemnations. Elizabeth could hear how much Sandy saw himself as a "learner, a curiosity seeker in life." Elizabeth's "co-dependence" began to be seen as an inherent quality of compassion and generosity that defined her. In divorce, they could begin to accept and even appreciate these differences. They no longer had to try to fit them into preconceived beliefs of how each needed to change to be in the marriage.

Both in their individual coaching meetings, where they were supported and challenged to engage in creating new conversations, and in their four-way coaching meetings, the new story began to take shape. Over the months that followed, they began the slow process of acceptance and letting go.

## IN THE MEANTIME: WHAT ABOUT THE DIVORCE?

Sometimes in this process, it seems as though the couple might reconcile. There were times when all of us, including Sandy and Elizabeth, hoped that might happen. We had the trust of their lawyers to take this break and see if that might be possible. They also worked concurrently with the financial neutral on the team to better understand their complex financial situation and to begin difficult conversations around money, a core conflict in their relationship. They also engaged a couples' therapist to work on their relationship. Sandy, however, could never trust a neutral therapist to understand him, and he eventually became disillusioned with the therapy. We ultimately all ended up in our collaborative seven-way meeting helping them formally end their marriage. The generosity that was Elizabeth was reflected in their settlement; the deep respect that Sandy was finally able to tap into was present as he became more open and transparent, and yes, grateful to her. They remain friends and supportive co-parents to this day.

## THE DISCLAIMER

Of course, we're aware that not all clients are like Sandy and Elizabeth who were both willing and able to take full advantage of what a collaborative interdisciplinary team process offers. Many are challenged by serious personality problems that create issues for the entire team. However, we do believe that having a licensed mental health professional who has additional mediation and collaborative training (a requirement for doing this work) creates the best possibility of change in this process. We see this happening even in the most challenging of cases.

Having his own divorce coach gives the client a distinct advantage in that the relationship that the client develops with his coach forms the basis for potential change. The coach works with the client to develop needed communication skills, manage stress and anxiety associated with divorce, and develop understanding for the spouse's viewpoint, giving the client the opportunity to participate in the process to the best of the client's ability. While this is not therapy, our goal is to make it as therapeutic as possible for all involved.

Looking back through this complex case, we believe certain elements were essential in the creation of their new, more adaptable story.

- The coaches constantly communicated with each other and built a trusting relationship.
- The coaches also communicated regularly with the rest of the team and kept them informed of emerging issues. Team members were provided with notes from four-way coach/client meetings.
- Coaches generally come from a "strength based" approach, and the work with Sandy and Elizabeth was no different. Peggy used *the Character Strengths survey VIA (Virtues in Action)* as a helpful way of identifying their strengths.
- Much of the work is done, of course, in individual sessions where many of the attitude shifts occur. In a coach model, all of this is time-limited and very focused on helping clients reach their stated goals while defining the changing family relationships going forward.
- In these individual coaching sessions, each client felt validated and "seen" in ways that they did not experience with each other. This proved to be a core piece in the deconstruction of their original stories in that the clients not only felt understood by their coaches but we could use that insight and bring it to our four-way meetings to help them "see" each other in a different way.
- We used a systems approach to understand the clients in their world with their unique history. Equally important, we utilized the unique strengths and expertise of our co-team members who provided a wealth of support and ideas that informed our work and made it possible to create real change even in the midst of chaos.
- In four-way meetings with clients, each coach looked for opportunities to demonstrate healthy behaviors and support the other coach, which prevented us from being pulled into the couple's

negative dynamic and taking sides.

- We also debriefed with each other after each four-way meeting, taking what had occurred and strategizing on how to utilize it going forward. This allowed us to build upon emerging new behaviors and insights and use those in reconstructing the clients' negative narratives.

Our stories do define us, but we are not at their mercy—no matter how real they seem at the beginning of the process. Stories can change, even in the worst of times. Given the opportunity to work with skilled professionals, we do not need to remain "stuck" with our defensive explanations but can realize this opportunity to create healthier relationships post-divorce. That's what coaches do.

Peggy Thompson, Ph.D., has been a licensed psychologist for 32 years, specializing in treating children and families. For over 20 years, she has been intensely involved in the divorce process in such roles as custody evaluator, special master, and high conflict counselor.

During the last 17 years, Dr. Thompson has led the development of the collaborative divorce process. She started teaching the collaborative divorce process in 1997, and she has contributed to the ongoing evolution of the process since that time. She is one of the founders and co-directors of Collaborative Divorce Associates in California. She is one of the co-founders of the International Academy of Collaborative Professionals and of Collaborative Divorce Trainings. She currently offers live trainings online as an affordable way for mental health professionals to gain a better understanding of the roles they can play to help families through collaborative practice.

Dr. Thompson has been published several times on the subject of collaborative practice. She and Dr. A. Rodney Nurse co-authored *Collaborative Divorce: A Humane, Interdisciplinary Approach*. Dr. Thompson also authored a chapter in *Innovations in Practice: A Source Book*, as well as *Collaborative Divorce: A New, Interdisciplinary Approach* in the American Journal of Family Law. She co-authored *Divorce: A Problem to be Solved, not a Battle to be Fought*. Dr. Thompson and Pauline Tesler co-authored *Collaborative Divorce*.

As a co-founder of the collaborative interdisciplinary team approach, Nancy J. Ross LCSW, BCD has worked for over 30 years with families and couples as they go through the difficulties and challenges of divorce.

She provides the support, guidance, and coaching couples need to help them minimize conflict and achieve the goals they have created for themselves and their children as they complete their divorce process. Whether serving as a divorce coach, communications specialist for trusts and estates, or mediator, she helps each individual be the best s/he can be during a difficult and trying time.

Ms. Ross is author of *Divorce: A Problem to be Solved; Not a Battle to be Fought* and numerous articles on collaborative practice. She is a recipient of the California Collaborative Practice Eureka Award, cofounder of the International Academy of Collaborative Professionals, a Collaborative Practice trainer, and a frequent presenter on the subjects of Collaborative divorce and Collaborative trusts and estates.

Ms. Ross' passion has always been focused on families. What makes them work? What keeps them from connecting? Finding the answers to these questions has been at the core her professional life. She never finds that it gets boring or stops being challenging. This work spurred her interest in helping create the collaborative interdisciplinary team concept. She enjoys helping families keep those connections at a time when they may least want to do so. Collaborative practice allows her to use her training and skills to make a difference in so many lives. And now, even at 80 years of age, she can't seem to stop doing it!

*There's a saying within legal circles that "criminal law deals with bad people at their best and family law deals with good people at their worst." People involved in domestic disputes are usually experiencing one of life's most stressful, emotional, and traumatic times. While it is difficult for everyone, certain clients are especially sensitive to the stress of divorce.*

*A client with an anxiety disorder will show symptoms that are not appropriate to the context. These folks might experience panic attacks. They might avoid or escape from uncomfortable situations. They may exhibit self-destructive behaviors. They may be consumed about what others think of them or assume that the worst result is inevitable.*

*Not only do these fears impact the anxious client's everyday life but they can also have devastating effects on a person going through a divorce. He may agree to anything just to get the divorce over with. He may not participate, causing a default to be entered against him. He may become so anxious that he abuses alcohol and drugs or participates in other destructive behaviors.*

*Therefore, it is even more important for divorces to be handled collaboratively where at least one client is highly anxious. The courtroom is no place for these people, and they benefit from the inclusion of a strong mental health professional on the collaborative team.*

## CULTIVATING EMOTIONAL SAFETY
## WITH THE HIGHLY ANXIOUS CLIENT
### BY YUVAL BERGER, MSW, RSW

"I need your help," Emma exclaimed, walking into my office. "My best friend, Kate, referred me to you. She told me that you did excellent work supporting her and Justin during their separation."

119

Emma was a petite woman with natural blond, straight hair. She could easily have been mistaken for a teenager, dressed in a feminine, flowered sundress and yellow sandals and clutching a small purse that could not have fit much more than her cell phone and keys.

Emma sat down on the couch, carefully observing the interior of my office. It appeared as if she was searching for familiar objects, looking at my books, art, and even plants. I felt that Emma's opening statement and her observations were an attempt to create a connection between us. Emma was searching for similarities between our lives as a way of assessing whether I could be a "safe" person to contain her vulnerability. Emma's distress was evident; her facial expressions and her demeanor suggested that she was under a considerable strain that she could barely manage. The dark circles under her eyes were the result of, as she said, her "chronic insomnia."

Her husband Martin was the one who initially contacted me by phone, explaining, "Emma was nervous and asked that I make the initial call to you. You were the facilitator in her best friend's divorce, so she felt most comfortable retaining you for our divorce."

He shared with me his reasons for leaving the marriage of 15 years. "We grew apart; the love was not there anymore." I noticed that his emotional narrative of the separation was excessively positive, simplistic, and disingenuous. When I asked Martin about Emma, he used contradictory adjectives, minimizing her response to the separation. For example, during the same brief telephone conversation, he told me, "Emma is doing really well, and she appreciates my decision." And also, "Last night, she couldn't control her anger. She pushed me away. Her angry outbursts can sometimes reach the point where I'm concerned she will become violent." Martin, as much as he tried to present Emma in an objective light, was downplaying her feelings, perhaps trying to distance himself from the emotional whirlwind his decision had triggered.

"Martin, what goals do you have for your divorce?" I asked.

"I want a quick and cheap resolution. I just want to be able to move on as soon as possible. I've been over this marriage for years," he explained, somewhat callously.

Soon after speaking with Martin, I contacted Emma to see how she was doing and to set an in-person meeting. Emma barely spoke during our telephone conversation, so rather than force conversation, I set a time for us to meet.

My gut feeling instructed me to ask Martin and Emma to come in for separate individual meetings. From my brief conversations with them, it seemed that Emma and Martin held two distinctively different narratives about their relationship breakdown and their reasons for ending it. Both narratives needed to be heard and acknowledged, and their stories, at this point, should not have been compared for their experiences to be fully accepted.

One of the most helpful schemes for conceptualizing how to support adults struggling with interpersonal problems is the model of attachment system activation and associated affect regulation strategies.[1] According to this model, when adults perceive a threat in their close relationship, their attachment system is activated in much the same way as in infancy. However, adults have a longer history of developmental experiences that influence the next stage of the process, namely, a determination whether an attachment figure is available and likely to be responsive. If the person determines that answer is "yes," she will use security-based strategies to seek comfort and emotional proximity with attachment figures. However, adults who appraise their environment as lacking in available and responsive attachment figures will experience a heightened sense of distress and will engage in two possible strategies. Those who anticipate that seeking closeness with another adult may result in some measure of felt security are likely to engage in hyperactivity attachment strategies, whereas those who believe that closeness seeking is impractical (i.e., would likely add more stress to their life) will engage in deactivating attachment strategies.[2] Each of these strategies requires a specific intervention approach in order to lay the foundation for effective working alliances that will eventually support the client during her separation process.

Divorce can disrupt or reaffirm a client's experience of emotional security or insecurity, as it pertains to one's close relationships on the deepest level. In this chapter, I describe the unique role of the collaborative divorce coach as a secure base when working with a client who presents with an anxious attachment style during relationship breakdown.

The idea of a CDC as a secure base has been valuable for my clinical work. While it makes intuitive sense, it is based on Ainsworth's important contribution to attachment theory, the secure base concept.[3] When a mother provides an atmosphere of safety, she raises the "child's threshold for fear of the unfamiliar." The CDC's availability, consistency, sensitivity, counsel, and responsiveness are what allow the client, in the midst of her relational crisis, to re-establish a sense of security in the process and possibly in future relationships. The attunement between the client's subjective experience of her separation and the CDC's deep understanding of the client's experiences results in the client experiencing *felt security*. Felt security is the underpinning of the collaborative process and what differentiates this process from its alternatives. The CDC is often, but not exclusively, the professional who is expected to engage with clients on this deep emotional level, and, therefore, is well positioned to serve as a secure base. The benefits for the clients from this experience are plenty, from immediate stress reduction and acceptance of help in engaging in the exploration of interests and options, to creativity and openness to trying new behaviors while being present in difficult negotiations.

Each and every client is different and unique, and therefore, the way in which they experience and react to the loss of their committed relationship is distinctive. The challenge for the CDC is to adjust her skills to her client's circumstances, personality, ability to self-regulate, and attachment style.

## SAFETY AT LAST

The collaborative process is about creating a brand-new experience of safety for the clients. This kind of safety provides an atmosphere for inspired guidance, while at the same time, giving the clients the courage to attempt new behavior when facing the emotional-psychological abyss often encountered at the termination of a close relationship. Although the safety in the process is primarily embedded in the collaborative principles of transparency, cooperation, team approach, and the withdrawal clause, it is the relationship between the professional and the client that nurtures the emotional experience of felt security. During the collaborative process, it is often the CDC who is expected to be attuned to the client's emotional experience and to facilitate her emotional regulation.

People who are hurt by people can repair their hurt by having a supportive, safe relationship with others. It is the experience of felt security which allows a client to calm her nervous system, self-sooth, explore options, make a decision pertaining to her future, and eventually, move on. Felt security is also critical in resetting a client's ability to think rationally, make good decisions, access creativity, use a "big picture" approach, and act empathically.

As previously mentioned, the experience of emotional safety or felt security is unique and different for each client and her attachment style. A hyperactivated attachment system requires a different conceptualization and intervention than that of a client who employs deactivation attachment system. Shavar and Hazan described adults with the hyperactivated attachment system as having anxious/preoccupied attachment style.[4] Although adults exhibiting hyperactivated attachment system seek approval and reassurance from others, this rarely relieves their self-doubt, feelings of powerlessness, and pessimism. In their relationships, adults with the hyperactivated attachment system experience a deep-seated feeling that they are going to be rejected, and this, in turn, causes worry and lack of trust.

Therefore, the main challenge for the CDC working with an adult with anxious attachment style is the formation of a secure relationship, especially since the client has recently experienced rejection in her primary relationship, regardless of whether the client is the one who initiated the separation.

## MORE THAN NEUTRALITY

At the end of my initial meeting with Emma, I suggested a two-coach process for her and Martin. I explained to her my rationale and that I would be referring him to a colleague, while I remained her coach during the process. It was my assessment that Emma would feel more secure in an aligned relationship, rather than in a process where she and Martin were being supported by one neutral coach.

Clinical research supports that people with anxious attachment styles might interpret neutral stances, statements, and facial expressions as threat cues.[5] An anxious person could mistakenly read the neutral expression as an indicator that the other person (be it a professional or a partner) does not understand her. This may lead the client to feel rejected and disappointed.

I have learned (through countless mistakes) that when I am the coach for the highly anxious client, I should avoid suggesting that "there are two sides to every breakup" or that "we should search for the win-win solution." These metaphors, although grounded in the best practices of conflict resolution, could be understood by the anxious client as an attempt to undermine her feelings.

I have noticed that my anxious clients feel supported when they experience me as continually attempting to understand their unique predicament and their stories. I try to engage in a dialogue with the client that accommodates, as much as possible, the client's subjective experience. During my individual meetings with Emma, I used a soothing tone, made eye contact, and often interrupted our communication with validation of her emotional experience. At the same time, I was carefully treading the fine line between supporting her subjective reality while avoiding blaming Martin exclusively for her predicament.

I described to Emma the principals of the collaborative process and promised her that the whole team and I would "have her back" while supporting her entire family. As soon as I used this metaphor, Emma's demeanor completely changed, her body relaxed, her shoulders dropped, and her eyes started to tear up. According to my assessment, Emma benefited from a CDC who provided her with an experience of calmness, validation, and emotional containment. I acted as an advocate who was able to relate to her emotional experience and be patient and available while setting proper boundaries and expectations. I shared my assessment of Emma's emotional vulnerability with the team, and, in particular, with her lawyer.

I referred Emma to a lawyer with whom I was familiar and who had an excellent reputation for supporting anxious clients.

## COMMUNICATION

Adults with an anxious attachment style tend to use many words to describe their hardship, yet their narrative can be confusing and tangential. It often lacks coherence and is based on unsupported generalities. Their description of life events is lacking in balance (often too negative) and tends to use catastrophic metaphors.[6]

Emma fit this description; her sentences were wordy and drawn-out, and I often found it challenging to follow her. Her description of her emotional state included adjectives that suggested that she was constantly in a state of crisis. For the CDC, this type of communication can be demanding on many levels. I found it challenging to discern what information was relevant to our process and which one of her worries (her children, finance, or the matrimonial home) was her main concern. They all seemed to be of the "highest priority." My initial tasks as Emma's CDC were to help her become coherent in her communication with Martin and her lawyer, help her identify her main concerns, and prepare her for our first four-way meeting.

I asked Emma to prioritize her concerns using a simple exercise. I provided her with cue cards and asked her to write down each worry on a separate card. Then I asked her to organize the cards so that the most important concern was placed close to her heart. This technique helped Emma recognize her main concern. It also helped me identify the main emotional theme which I would need to help her express in our joint meetings. Emma's main emotional theme was her experience of powerlessness.

Emma's written communication and phone messages were a growing concern to me. Emma wrote lengthy emails, copying the whole team, including detailed descriptions of her feelings, her memories, and what she perceived as "red flags." I knew that Emma's story needed to be heard in full; nevertheless, I was concerned about the financial implications of her sending lengthy emails to me and her lawyer, as well as the possibility of splitting between team members.

Recognizing that Emma needed to tell her story more than once, I suggested she write down her stories as a memoir and keep a diary where she could record, on a daily basis, her thoughts, insights, and painful memories. In addition, I advised Emma not to share her painful feelings with Martin in either emails or text messages. I informed her that such actions would trigger her feelings of betrayal and would cause her to feel unsafe. I explained that Martin could not give her the emotional validation she needed at this time and that she was better of seeking support from her friends and family. In preparation for our coming four-way meetings, I coached Emma on how to be concise with her description of her emotional experience and how to focus on one topic at the time while avoiding pleading.

One of Emma's complaints about the four-way meetings was her experience of not being heard and understood by Martin and his coach. Often, in our regular debrief after the four-way meetings, Emma protested that the meeting was unbalanced and that she was not getting equal "airtime." This was in spite of my own observation, where I found Emma, at times, dominating the meetings and demanding to be heard, while struggling to listen to Martin's needs. In an attempt to mitigate this perception, I offered that the other coach and I would monitor the time allocated to each party to discuss their agenda items.

## HOPE

Offering hope to a distraught client is one of my responsibilities as the CDC, and, yet, when working with the anxious client, the facilitation of hope is not without its challenges. According to Daniel, an anxious client tends to heighten her stress in the face of assistance and is inclined to think negatively about her future. The intensification of negative emotional states has an expressive function and serves to maximize the possibility of receiving the wanted care.

The problem with this approach is that it requires the anxious client to scan for potential disappointment, which might push her to become rather pessimistic and distrustful about any solution for her predicaments. Stan Tatkin described the anxious person as "allergic to hope."[7] Contrary to the common belief that hope can serve as a motivation to overcome a difficult situation, for the anxious person, hope can be a reminder of potential disappointment and the ultimate abandonment. For the coach, the negative outlook and the perceived refusal to "get better" prove to be a real obstacle in ensuring the advancement of the process. It also might impact the relationship between the client and the coach, as well as the relationships among team members.

In my one-on-one meetings with Emma, I prepared her for the ambivalent feelings she might experience as the process moved forward. I reassured her that if we reached an agreement, it was by no means an attempt to dilute her emotional experience or to undermine it. Providing Emma with a personal emotional roadmap for the process proved to be a powerful and effective tool. Emma cherished the explanation of the discordance between the progression of the process and her emotional experience. Knowing what to expect in our meeting and having my understanding, helped her adjust her expectations accordingly. I noticed that her safety and trust in the process increased when she was allowed to describe the depth of her emotions while gently navigating her way through the collaborative process with my support. When her feelings were at odds with the agreements we made or with the pace of the meetings, I reassured her that her feelings would not be compromised and that they would never be negotiated.

At the end of our process, when Emma and I met to debrief the outcome of our work, Emma shared with me that my assurance to never negotiate her feelings was a mantra she had adopted through our difficult meetings and negotiations. The mantra helped her feel entitled to her subjective experience while conversing with Martin about the future of their children and their co-parenting relationship.

## THE ANXIOUS CLIENT AND THE TEAM

The coach for the anxious client is responsible for being the bridge between the client's subjective experience and the team. Explaining the client's emotional process and her perceived helplessness to the team could lessen the concern about the client's

127

motivation to resolve her separation and move forward. Emma's melodramatic presentation, ambivalent stance, and helplessness proved to be confusing not only to me but also to the collaborative team. The other professionals raised concerns about Emma's readiness to engage in meaningful collaborative negotiations in our team debriefs, including the risk that Emma's ambivalent posture could slow down the process and eventually lead to Martin's loss of trust in the team.

The challenge for the coach (and the team) is not to confuse the "surface" with the reality that lies beneath it. In other words, the challenge is not to take a client's helplessness at face value, but rather, as a defense against a deep-rooted fear of perceived abandonment. CDCs (and lawyers) are at risk of falling into the trap of rescuing the client as a way of providing a safe process when working with an anxious client. Yet, when we are tempted into playing this role, we might lose sight of the client's strength and the chance to provide her with a genuinely felt security.

## SUMMARY

In this chapter, I described my work with Emma. Emma's state of mind, behavior, and self-regulations indicated that she is an individual with an anxious attachment style. My work with her as a CDC was aimed, among other things, at helping her feel "psychologically held" enough to be able to self-sooth and to empower her through the collaborative process.

Emma and Martin completed the collaborative process after six months of negotiation. In my last meeting with Emma, she revealed, "This process has been one of the most emotionally agonizing and yet transformative processes I have ever been through."

"What did you find to be the most helpful in our work together, Emma?"

She thought for a moment, her eyes filled with tears, and then she replied, "When you said to me that my feelings will not be negotiated and that you will always have my back."

---

[1] Mikulincer, M., & Shaver, P. R. (2007). *Attachment in Adulthood: Structure, Dynamics, and Change.* Guilford Press.

[2] Mallinckrodt, B., Daly, K., & Wang, C. C. D. (2009). An Attachment Approach to Adult Psychotherapy. *Attachment Theory and Research in Clinical Work With Adults*, 234-268.

[3] Ainsworth, M. D. S. (1967). Infancy in Uganda: Infant Care and the Growth of Love.

[4] Hazan, C., & Shaver, P. (1987). Romantic love conceptualized as an attachment process. *Journal of personality and social psychology*, *52*(3), 511.

[5] Chris Fraley, R., Niedenthal, P. M., Marks, M., Brumbaugh, C., & Vicary, A. (2006). Adult Attachment and the Perception of Emotional Expressions: Probing the Hyperactivating Strategies Underlying Anxious Attachment. *Journal of Personality*, *74*(4), 1163-1190.

Sheaffer, B. L., Golden, J. A., & Averett, P. (2009). Facial Expression Recognition Deficits and Faulty Learning: Implications for Theoretical Models and Clinical Applications. *International Journal of Behavioral Consultation and Therapy*, *5*(1), 31.

Yoon, K. L., & Zinbarg, R. E. (2008). Interpreting Neutral Faces as Threatening is a Default Mode for Socially Anxious Individuals. *Journal of Abnormal Psychology*, *117*(3), 680.

[6] Daniel, S. (2014). *Adult Attachment Patterns in a Treatment Context: Relationship and Narrative*. Routledge.

[7] Tatkin, S. (2011). Allergic to Hope: Angry Resistant Attachment and a One-Person Psychology Within a Two-Person Psychological System. *Psychotherapy in Australia*, *18*(1), 30.

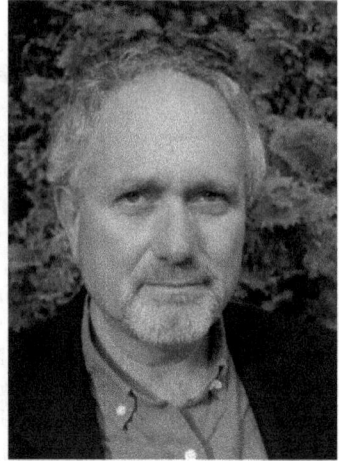

Yuval Berger, MSW, RSW, brings with him 25 years of clinical experience as a relationship and child therapist with special expertise in supporting couples through the dissolution of their intimate relations. Over the years, he has practiced as a divorce coach, child specialist, family therapist, and a trainer. Mr. Berger joined the Vancouver, BC, collaborative group in 2002, and, since then, has been an active member, supporting and promoting the interdisciplinary team approach. He is an associate of the Collaborative Center in Vancouver, Canada, which is a joint private venture of family lawyers and mental health professionals all practicing collaborative law.

The International Academy of Collaborative Professionals (IACP) elected Mr. Berger to its board of directors for the 2012-15 terms. Mr. Berger has taught basic and advanced interdisciplinary CP courses in Canada, England, Scotland, the US, and Israel. He has presented in numerous IACP forums in North America and in Europe and has taught in the IACP Institute in the US and Australia.

When offering advanced training, Mr. Berger focuses on expanding professional knowledge about the possibilities for couples to move from an intimate relationship into a co-parenting relationship and the interplay between psychology and the field of conflict resolution. He brings his knowledge and experience in using attachment theory to facilitate a better understanding of a couple's experience through their separation.

*When an emotional bomb is dropped on a client, the collaborative team should immediately come together to give the client the support she needs so she can eventually proceed in a productive manner. This is yet another example of how the mental health professional is an invaluable member of the collaborative team. Many attorneys and financial professionals don't know what to do when a client receives extremely upsetting news or when she becomes extremely emotional. The mental health professional, who is trained in how to deal with these pitfalls, can guide the team in the appropriate way to proceed when a client's world is blown apart.*

## HOW TO TELL A WOMAN SHE IS NO LONGER A WIFE: THE IRREDUCIBLE MINIMUM
### BY ANNE PURCELL, PH.D.

You are working in a one-coach model. The venue is your office. Meeting number two is starting, and you are welcoming your team and clients. As you begin to introduce agenda item number one, you notice the wife, Bridget, nervously fidgeting in her chair. She is a well-dressed woman in her thirties. Despite the stress of her divorce, she always seems in control, so you are surprised to see her looking nervous. As you make your introductions, she looks you in the eye and waves her hand a bit, clearly wanting to say something.

"Bridget, is there something you need before we get started?" you politely ask.

With a strong yet shaky voice, looking deeply into her husband's eyes, Bridget begins. "I'd like to pause the collaborative process. I have realized that our marriage is not over for me. I have come to this meeting to ask Mike if he will consider reconciling our relationship."

This is news to everyone. The lawyers shuffle papers and say nothing.

Mike, a polished businessman, immediately looks away. He is still for a moment that seems an eternity. A long, heavy silence envelops the room. Finally, with his eyes looking forward but focused nowhere in particular, he slowly says, "Reconciliation will not be possible."

Before he can continue, Bridget interrupts, "But Mike, we have so much together, how can you just throw that all away. I love—"

"Natasha is pregnant." Mike interrupts. "We're getting married. I didn't want you to find out this way."

Stunned, Bridget looks Mike directly in the eyes and says, "Natasha? My best friend?"

An emotional tsunami has hit, and it will be your job to navigate it. All of your preparation for this meeting does not matter now. Your agenda for the meeting is in tatters. Your colleagues are searching your face for clues on how to proceed. What do you do?

## TRIAGE

First, switch gears. Adjust your thinking from process management to crisis control. There will be no meeting now. Be nimble in thought and movement, decisive but unobtrusive. Ask everyone except Bridget to leave the room. Ask her if she'd like her lawyer to stay. Don't allow anyone in again until she has recovered her composure. This will take as long as it takes.

Second, find your case notes, even if they are not close at hand. You will need them, especially the page that lists her goals and interests.

Third, manage your colleagues. This was unplanned, so no one will know what to do in this moment. They will be milling in the halls, wondering what will happen next. You all know that collaborative teams work best when they have invested in preparation. But what do you do when no amount of preparation can prepare you for an emotional curve ball? Convene an emergency team meeting, stressing that you do not want to leave Bridget alone for long because it is your priority now to be with her. Ask Mike's lawyer to stay with him. Tell them it will take as long as it takes. Give Mike's lawyer some advice on how to manage the husband and to not allow him to leave. He may be needed later.

Quietly alert your administration staff that a difficult meeting is occurring. You know they will be sensitive because you have trained them to respect emotion as well as process but remind them of the fundamentals. Talk in low voices. If the office kitchen is near the meeting rooms, keep dish noises to a minimum. There should be no beeping microwaves, chatter, laughter, or food smells from the lunchroom. Avoid any signs of "life as usual." For this woman, on this day, nothing about life is usual. If there is nothing to eat except office kitchen fare, send someone out to buy something to nibble on for both meeting rooms. This is going to take a while and some people like to eat while they think. This is as important as ensuring both clients' privacy by never leaving them in rooms with glass walls or doors where their grief and shock will be on display.

## HOLD THE SPACE

Go and be with Bridget. If she is sitting, sit beside her. If she is standing, stand with her, shoulder-to-shoulder. You might look out the window together, but avoid the physical and emotional confrontation of too much eye contact just now. Just be there with her.

If she rages, let her. The client who externalizes is usually easier to manage than the one whose body doubles over in silent screams. Ultimately, but not now, challenge her if she threatens to "see him in court." Remind her of her own goals of protecting her family from litigation. It would be easy to entrench her in this position now, but this is not why you do this work, is it?

If she is silent or stunned or unreachable, say nothing. When she asks, "What will I do now?"; "What will I tell the kids?"; "How will I go on without him?" do not provide any answers. Understand that your job is not to identify solutions or to "fix it." This is her job, but that will come later.

Add nothing new to the conversation. Rather, just loop her own thoughts back to her by saying things like, "We'll have to figure out something to tell the kids, won't we?" Just help her get to "yes." This is the first step toward her future, and really, it's all you can achieve in this moment.

She could nod her head deeply. Or cry. Or stand very still. If she asks what you would do, don't respond directly. Instead, remind her, "This is about you, not me. You are what is important now." Remind yourself that you are not there to impact an outcome but to guide her toward hers. Just hold the space.

## SHIFT THE FOCUS

Know what to do when she repeats herself, keeps circling back to what she was talking about a half hour ago, or starts bargaining with her grief again ("If only"; "I'll try harder to make it work"; "He could change his mind"). With an intuition that was borne of many moments like this, you will know when it is time to begin to shift her focus.

You will do this by guiding her to recall her goals. Your notes that list her goals and interests will be at hand, but you probably won't need them to jog your memory. Her goals are likely as familiar to you as they now are to her. Together, you have identified, defined, and questioned them so many times. But, if her goals represent her future, and right now, she is revisiting her past, simply put your notes on the table. This is why you needed them. It was for this moment. She needs to *see* them to remember what her future looks like because all she can see now is her past. Hand her a pen and tell her to rewrite them if necessary. Guide her from emotion to reason. Help her remember her irreducible truth.

## REVISIT HER GOALS

Now, you will draw on the work you carefully and skillfully did with her weeks before when you helped her identify her goals. Among the many broad, hazy goals, the mélange of previously unarticulated desires and unspoken hopes, a truth emerged.

You helped her articulate one goal that would set her future life's course, should she dare to wish for it. Don't remind her of it as though you are the knower-of-all-things; rather, lead her to that part for herself. She will recall that really, there is only one thing she desires in a relationship and that is to prioritize her partner and to have him prioritize her. For her, it is about putting the relationship before everything else. Without this, she would rather have no relationship at all.

This is her irreducible minimum.

You know this because she told you so herself. Use her name, and ask her if you have remembered this correctly. When she tells you yes, and she will because you didn't make it up, you are only telling her what she told you in the first place. She will realize, probably not for the first time, that this relationship is not good for her. She may quietly weep now because she knows her marriage is over. Allow silence to descend. Hold the space, and be still in the moment.

How do you tell a woman she is no longer a wife? You don't. Remain quiet. Your skill will have guided her to her new truth. Words are superfluous now.

As this happens, allow her to loop back into her grief as if it's the first time she has heard it. Expect denial, anger, bargaining, and sadness. Expect all of these or none of them. The experience is unique to her, and so too will be her reaction. Just wait.

## KNOW YOUR PLACE

Be careful with the information you have. If she asks, tell her what you know. But don't tell her the hurtful details that will only create demons in her mind. Don't give her the answers to the questions she has not asked. You might know some of the sordid details, but if she doesn't ask, don't tell. Now is not the time.

She may need to ask him the questions herself and see his face when he tells her. She may never want to know. That will be up to her to decide, and her choices may be different from yours. Don't assume you know what's best for her. You don't. In this moment, she may not either. But time and space will bring her enough clarity to ask a new set of questions.

Don't judge her for not being further along this path; for agreeing to a divorce and then having second thoughts; for lacking clarity and not being certain of her own mind. This woman's decision to stay in her marriage for so long as she did is hers alone. This is about her perspective, not yours. Park your judgment at the door, and be alert to your own triggers or potential for transference.

Do not present her with a silver lining. Never say "at least": "At least you finally have the answers you were seeking"; "At least the decision has been made for you now." There is no "at least." Saying so is unhelpful.

## BE ALERT TO YOUR CLIENTS' NEEDS

Help her manage this moment. If you don't know what she needs right now, ask. Walk with her to the bathroom if the route there means she has to pass the room where her husband waits.

She may recover enough to decide she wants to continue with the meeting. You know this is not a good idea, but let her decide. If she wants to meet with her husband first, ask her if she wants you to be present. It is very likely she will, and when you do, you will be there for both her *and* him. This is difficult for him, too. They need you to reaffirm the tenets of respect and their common goals and to model for them why they chose to do this collaboratively in the first place. You are the only team member who can work with both clients like this.

Later, when she is leaving, don't initiate it yourself, but be ready for her to reach out and embrace you. Sometimes this happens. If it does, embrace her back. Understand that if she seeks human connection, it's a good sign that her mind is connected sufficiently to her body so that she can act on this. It means her mind is reeling less. You have facilitated this.

## RESET THE COURSE

Your responsibility is to give your team members the information they need to make process decisions. Convene a team debrief immediately after the clients have left. With their counsel, strategize about how to keep the process on course, albeit with altered timing. Discuss process options. Remember what you learned of her today in her unguarded moments is for you alone. Treat this with the utmost discretion.

When your team leaves and you reenter your office, demonstrate this discretion again. The office staff need not search your face for clues of this woman's most personal and raw self. Be the guardian of her privacy. Respect her grief.

It goes without saying that you will call her tomorrow to check in on her and to begin to plan her next steps, however altered they may be. Feed this information back to your colleagues, and together, you will move the process forward.

When you get home, blend into the tone of your house the same way you blended into her space today. Avoid bringing the weight of your day with you. Your life is not her life, but you were with her on one of the worst days of her life. This was a privilege, and you recognize it at as such. Cook your dinner, chew your food slowly, and think about what you contributed—to her, to your team, to society. You helped a family today.

That is your irreducible minimum.

Anne Purcell, Ph.D., is the founder and CEO of Resolution Partners in Queensland, Australia, an innovative alternative to traditional dispute resolution services for families experiencing family breakdown and transition. Dr. Purcell did her graduate studies in psycholinguistics at Harvard and the University of Queensland in Australia. Her interest in the psychology of conflict, communication, and learning is a primary influence. Dr. Purcell's main areas of expertise are educational psychology, interest-based negotiation, mediation, collaborative practice, and corporate and professional training.

In addition to her practice, Dr. Purcell is a registered teacher, media presenter and commentator, former prime-time TV host, and national and international speaker. Her training for professionals focuses on psycho-legal professional development, what neuroscience can teach us about managing conflict, alternative dispute resolution, collaborative practice and parenting coordination training, and child development outcomes for children following family breakdown.

Dr. Purcell is a former academic. She continues to teach at universities in addition to regularly delivering keynote and plenary addresses for academic audiences and professional seminars for lawyers, barristers, and collaborative professionals around the world.

Dr. Purcell sits on the committee of Queensland Collaborative Law and is the sole southern hemisphere member of the training faculty for the IACP. She was a co-founder of the Interdisciplinary Queensland Collaborative Law Training Committee, the most prolific interdisciplinary collaborative law training team in the state. As a counterpoint to her teaching and public engagements, Dr. Purcell is one of the busiest non-legal collaborative professionals and mediators in her region.

*The end of a marriage is akin to the death of a loved one. Spouses experience the five stages of grief—denial, anger, bargaining, depression, and acceptance—as they learn to live without the relationship. Divorcing spouses go through the stages at different times, which can be especially hard on the client who travels more slowly through the stages.*

*The way that a couple chooses to "uncouple" can mean the difference between a devastating breakup that destroys the individuals and the family and a healthy, therapeutic split in which the individuals grow and the family is restructured.*

*Understanding the neuroscience principles of attachment styles, emotional regulations, and brain arousal helps professionals guide their divorcing clients through a healthy, secure uncoupling that promotes the best interests of the individuals and the families. This "secure uncoupling" leaves the clients physically, emotionally, psychologically, and mentally healthier. It enables the clients to successfully close the door on their married lives and to open the door to new, happier beginnings.*

## "SECURE UNCOUPLING": HEALTHY DIVORCE
## THROUGH THREE NEUROSCIENCE PRINCIPLES
### BY JOY A. DRYER, PH.D.

When couples come into my office for therapy or a divorce consultation, we often end up discussing how and why they fell in love. Over 40 years in practice, I have often asked myself, "Is there a healthy way to fall out of love?" I now firmly believe that there is. I have repeatedly seen individuals transform through the process of "uncoupling[1]" to be far less distressed than they were as a couple.

This chapter explains what I have learned. The journey through "uncoupling" is most transformative when you keep in mind three core principles rooted in modern neuroscience. I call these principles the "ABCs of transformative divorce."

First comes "A" for attachment style. Understanding how and why you connect with others is key to seeing why you fall in, and out, of love. Next is "B" for brain arousal. How you perceive safety or threat directly impacts how you react moment-to-moment and can help explain many key reactions within your relationships. Lastly, I discuss what I call "consistent emotional regulation," the "C." This final section addresses your ability to predict interpersonal interactions and resolve conflict.

My experience has proven that if you are patient and ask probing questions about who you are and what you want, you can come out of a divorce more self-aware and happier. You can transform the pain of the divorce process by learning a better way to become your fullest self. The ABCs of this transformative divorce process are rooted in research at the cutting edge of interpersonal neuroscience. Your journey through a transformative divorce to resolution, to a goal of "secure functioning uncoupling," involves your deepening understanding of yourself no matter where you are along the arc of your divorce journey.

*Know Thyself* or *Gnothi Seauton*
(Greek: γνῶθι σεαυτόν)
~ Delphic maxim inscribed in the pronaos
(forecourt) of the Temple of Apollo at Delphi

### PSYCHOLOGY 101: WHERE WE STARTED

How you first get connected to intimate others offers an important foundation for how you can disconnect from them. From the moment a baby opens her eyes, she attempts to connect to her caretaker. Through a gazillion interactions, a human baby's brain learns what to expect from her adult caretakers. These interaction patterns become internal expectations remembered, or imprinted, in each baby's brain. Thus, as babies, we all learn to manage emotional experiences through increasingly complex brain neurocircuitry called "internal working models" (IWMs).[2]

These IWMs from infancy lay the foundation for: a) how comfortable you feel being close or distant from another person; b) how you regulate your emotions, i.e. how easily your feelings get aroused and how well you inhibit feelings as necessary; and c) how your brain assesses safety or threat in the environment. IWMs can remain relatively consistent from infancy through adulthood and form the basis of attachment styles, which reflect the predominant blueprint of how you bond, or connect, to others.

Thus, attachment styles, starting with the initial ABC building blocks of IWMs, are part of the larger picture of how your brain works. Because of the brain's inherent neuroplasticity, IWMs can shift via therapy or training, and you can rewire the neural circuitry of your brain.

## A IS FOR ATTACHMENT STYLES

In the 1960s and '70s, child psychologists began to describe how babies connect and bond with others based upon their earliest experiences with their primary caretaker(s).[3] In the table at the end of this chapter are the four attachment styles commonly described in the psychology literature as "secure" and "insecure" attachment.[4]

Styles of attaching with others, as well as hormone release processes, affect everyone's brain and nervous system development. So how you respond to the stress of divorce and how you adjust post-divorce reflects how you regulate your emotions, as well as your attachment style.[5] See if you recognize one style that predominates for you in this table, which offers a simplified structure of the integration of the ABCs.

Biological anthropologist Helen Fisher's three-brain-system research shows attachment in the larger context of three phases of how our bodies, brains, and hormones are built for love, which ensures continuation of our species.[6] These three brain systems are not necessarily connected to one another.

In Fisher's system, lust is the craving for sexual satisfaction. Elevated dopamine drives up testosterone. This helped our ancestors bed any range of partners to start the mating process.

Romantic attraction/love is high in dopamine and norepinephrine and low in serotonin. The elation and obsession of "being in love" enabled our ancestors to focus their time and energy on one individual, thus preserving precious mating time and energy.

And lastly, Fisher believes that the biological need for attachment evolved to loving one mate long enough to raise a child for the first few years. The "feel good" hormones, oxytocin and vasopressin, give you a feeling of calm, peace, and security, and help you tolerate that long-term mate.

Many who decide to divorce may have gotten along well with partners for the first two phases. The longer-term attachment phase is more challenging, especially when it shifts yet again in the "gray" years (over age 50), often after children are gone and more existential concerns enter regarding "Who am I?" and "What am I doing in the time I have left?"

## B IS FOR BRAIN AROUSAL

Each of these attachment styles gradually becomes organized around different ways of regulating emotions and biases for how our brain works. Our brains are wired to reduce threat and to seek safety.[7] Current research has also tracked how Bowlby's IWMs describe the self-regulatory variations responsible for attachment styles.[8]

When you feel secure in the world, you have freedom to be flexible with your thoughts and emotions. Because of high self-awareness and a capacity to regulate your emotions, you can make quick repairs after misattunements with your partner.

Growing up with a more "insecure" attachment style results in greater difficulty regulating high and low feelings mostly because a caretaker was unclear, had trouble soothing or calming down baby when upset, or stimulated her in age-inappropriate ways that the baby could not manage emotionally.

Anxious and avoidant attachment styles show almost opposite triggers to emotional distress. If anxious and focused on the other, her brain feels more threatened when detecting imminent separation or rejection. She can get easily excited with up-regulated emotions, and her main defense is to fight back. She can "feel, but not deal."

A person who dismisses and avoids her need for closeness and intimacy has a brain that detects threat when feeling as if her partner intrudes into her space or tries to control her. She is more likely to down-regulate her emotions and withdraw. So her main defense is flight. It is more natural for her to think logically and "deal, but not feel."

When a baby's earliest experiences of connection and attachment are not just unpredictable, but frightening, such a person's feelings and thoughts can become disorganized. This may result in great difficulty regulating high and low feelings. This can result in primitive feelings of losing yourself or your partner. She can feel emotionally tossed about as if in a storm, with difficulty finding a safe spot to rest. Her main defense may be to freeze or to fade.

## C IS FOR CONSISTENT EMOTION REGULATION

Your body already knows that transitioning out of marriage is experienced as a major life stress and as a threat to wellbeing.[9] Research has shown a clear mind-brain-body connection. Some divorcees self-medicate with drugs or alcohol. Many have sleep troubles. In a large meta-analysis study examining the association between divorce and all-cause mortality of 6.5 million people in 11 countries, 23% more separated or divorced adults died earlier (more men than women) than did their married counterparts.[10]

Remaining too emotionally connected to your ex is detrimental to your physical and emotional health. For example, people who have high anxiety about their relationships, are hypersensitive to relationship loss, and remain attached to their exes, show some increased risk for greater blood pressure reactivity.[11]

Those who have a hard time distancing themselves from these difficult psychological experiences show excessive cardiovascular reactivity leading over time to greater cardiovascular problems.[12] Research has shown that too much on-going attention to an ex results in impaired immune responses in a significant number of participants.[13]

So how do you protect yourself from divorce taking a toll on your health? Work toward a secure uncoupling. That is, as you

143

uncouple, your capacity for secure functioning will involve a range of both internal and external adjustments, as I will now highlight.

> Be the change you seek... *As a man changes his own nature, so does the attitude of the world change towards him.... A wonderful thing it is and the source of our happiness. We need not wait to see what others do.*
>
> ~ Mahatma Gandhi

## GOAL OF SECURE UNCOUPLING

Your physical and mental healths are less at risk when you uncouple more securely. Physically, good self-care is essential, including eating, sleeping, and exercising well. Activities like yoga or meditation can slow down your nervous system and even help you concentrate.

Emotionally, this internal process of separating and uncoupling during divorce features similar characteristics as secure attachment when in a relationship. When you can have a healthy, secure, functioning uncoupling, you increase your ability to have a transformative divorce. That is, your divorce journey can result in greater self-knowledge and more enriched happiness as you emerge from your divorce than you had going into it.

With emotional and physical risk post-divorce, you can earn transformation security with some specific self-awareness measures.

One of the major psychological adjustments all divorcees have to make post-divorce is some reorganization of sense of self.[14] Romantic breakups are associated with immediate persistent decreases in "self-concept clarity."[15] This is because, when married, we understand who we are as a person in relationship to our partner.[16]

Another function of attachment to a specific other is co-regulation of emotions.[17] When we co-regulate securely with a partner, the goal is a physiological homeostasis. However, when divorcing, we conclude that our attachment styles and brain biases were mismatched to some degree. For example, those with attachment anxiety are often emotionally hyper-activated, repeatedly seeking connection or closeness. Those with a more avoidant attachment style down-regulate emotions in an effort to deactivate and minimize distress.[18]

Other internal self-adjustments include redefining self-worth and readjusting roles, maybe as a single parent, with in-laws, with friends, with co-workers, etc. As post-divorcees, we can increase a sense of wellbeing as we recover our independent sense of self.[19] We can get greater clarity regarding who we are now.

Some basic self-care steps are to cultivate self-kindness and self-compassion, i.e. to love yourself.[20] Remind yourself of your common humanity. Use affirmations if that helps you. Remind yourself that others have divorced, just like you, and have survived. Even thrived! Your kids will likely do well if you do well.

Those with anxious attachment styles who stay focused on their exes show difficult post-divorce adjustment.[21] Those who brood, make over-generalizations, or engage in negative self-talk have a more difficult transition.[22]

Separating yourself from your ex happens internally. Avoid ruminating, or emotional journal writing, on every little detail of your relationship with your ex. Such ruminations increase your risk for mood disturbances.[23] Instead, look for meaning in your experiences. Thus, as you reset your internal boundary between you and your ex, your freed-up brain resources can now be used constructively elsewhere.

Forgiving your ex is even deeper work.[24] To do so may mean putting yourself in the other's shoes to understand fully his/her perspective. You may feel it means letting go of your wish for blame, revenge, to win, or to be right. This "giving up" can include grief, loss, shame, disappointment, loneliness, or mourning.[25]

This mourning process can help transform you toward earned security. One way to work through and out of it is to use a controlled writing exercise. In his study, Sbarra worked to help those who brooded, those who got into their own head or overly focused on dark feelings, and thus stayed stuck in pain.[26] Instead, he structured controlled writing in a concrete, non-emotional manner regarding how the person spent her time. This approach can tap into your ability to self-actualize, to be positively effective in the world, and to redefine and to reorganize positive self-concepts.

Social Baseline Theory suggests that social relationships, specifically another person's presence, reduce the metabolic load on the brain.[27] With increased social support, your brain lowers its threat vigilance to the environment.

Research has shown that greater marital satisfaction results in better physical and psychological wellbeing later in life.[28] However, a romantic relationship is not the only source of emotional and physical support. Friends and family provide a myriad of social connections deemed important for longevity and healthy aging.[29]

You can reach out to friends and family, as well as choose professionals whom you trust, to be reliable supports. Hence, even when you may experience yourself with an insecure attachment style, you can earn security by coupling up in a secure functioning relationship with family, friends, work colleagues, etc. who bear the hallmarks grounded in the essential values that will help you understand yourself well enough to learn from past missteps and walk into the future.

These are five fundamental characteristics to seek out in your next relationship. These will help you feel that you've earned your secure transformation of uncoupling, closer and closer to resolution, which involves mourning (grief and loss) and some forgiveness.

1. Security [feel safe with each other];
2. Sensitivity [respond to other's needs];
3. Justice and fairness [repair conflict quickly];
4. Collaboration [put your relationship first]; and
5. True mutuality [what's equally good, or bad, for both partners].[30]

With your new, or enhanced, self-knowledge and your sense of securely transformed uncoupling, you can heighten your awareness of how to find and to sustain a securely functioning relationship in the future.

Here are guidelines to keep self-awareness a priority in your next relationship:

1. Control your emotions (supports empathy and taking multiple perspectives);
2. Your brain seeks novelty (increases dopamine and romance);
3. Make affectionate comments daily; and
4. Stay in touch. Regular sex and kissing boost oxytocin (attachment), lower cholesterol, reduce cortisol (stress and anxiety), lower blood pressure, and boost memory.[31]

## CONCLUSION

You can, with mindful focus, learn enough about yourself in the three ABC areas I've discussed: attachment styles, brain biases, and consistent emotion regulation. You can use your divorce experiences to transform your life for the better. You can learn from past errors so you do not repeat missteps going forward. Thus, you can transform an unhealthy attachment to your ex into a healthy uncoupling, which can help you reach resolution with your past and open avenues for your enriched future happiness.

> *Out beyond ideas of wrongdoing and rightdoing, there is a field. I'll meet you there. When the soul lies down in that grass, the world is too full to talk about . . .*
>
> ~ Mevlana Jelaluddin Rumi - 13th c.

## SYSTEMS INTEGRATION: ATTACHMENT, EMOTION REGULATION, BRAIN AROUSAL

| ATTACHMENT STYLE | RELATIONSHIP WITH PARTNER [as adult] ~Primary attachment figure (1) ~Wish to be connected/ intimate | EMOTION REGULATION ~Self-regulation of emotions ~Self Agency | BRAIN BIASES, SELF (3) AROUSAL + DEFENSES ~Safety versus threat |
|---|---|---|---|
| SECURE [ANCHOR] (2) Goldilocks: "Just Right" | ~Secure as individuals ~Willing & able to experience distance & intimacy w/out losing personal autonomy. | ~High self-awareness + capacity for self-regulation makes quick repair more possible after misattunement | ["I'm OK. You're OK".] ~Excitatory & inhibitory feedback loops well-balanced. ~Relative absence of defense |
| ANXIOUS/ PREOCCUPIED [WAVE] (2) Goldilocks: "Too hot/ too much | ~Generous & giving ~Focus on caretaking of others ~Willing to please ~Can be high maintenance | ~Fears separation, rejection, hurt ~Regulates self via others' acceptance ~Can feel like "loses" oneself ~Can "feel, not deal" | ["I'm in pain. What are you gonna do about it".] ~Easily excited ~Bias to up-regulate MAIN DEFENSE: Fight |
| DISMISSING/ AVOIDANT [ISLAND] (2) Goldilocks: "Too cold/ too little" | ~Independent, self-reliant ~Good boundaries ~Low maintenance | ~Fears too much intimacy ~Can feel intruded upon/controlled ~Can "deal, not feel" | ["I'm OK. Don't worry about me."] ~Slow burn before excited ~Bias to down regulate MAIN DEFENSE: Flight, withdraw |
| DISORGANIZED/ [STORM] (4) Goldilocks: Vacillates between "Too little" & "Too much" and "Too hot" & "Too cold," even simultaneously. | ~Intensely experience the here-and-now ~Loving can zero in on other. ~Self-Other boundary hard to keep ~High maintenance | ~ Hard to regulate high & low feelings. Emotional regulation can feel tossed about like in a storm ~Fears both separation & intrusion ~Connection is unpredictable | ["I'm in worse pain than you. I'm overwhelmed. I'm falling apart."] ~Easily detects threat, external [distrustful] & internal [falling apart] ~ Emotion brain [limbic system] can disorganize rational brain [frontal lobe] MAIN DEFENSE: Freeze. Fade. |

(1) Bowbly, J. (1988)
(2) Tatkin, S. (2011)
(3) Categories adapted from George, C. & West, M. (2001)
(4) Holmes, B.M. & Lyons-Ruth, K. (2006)

---

[1] Vaugh, D. (1976). Uncoupling. Turning Points in Intimate Relationships. Oxford Univ. Press. NY

[2] Bretherton, I. & Munholland, K. (1999). Internal working models in attachment: A construct revisited. *In handbook of attachment theory*, 89-111. Guilford.

[3] Ainsworth, M., Blehar, M., Waters, E., & Wall, S. (1978). Patterns of attachment: A psychological study of the strange situation. Hillsdale, MJ: Lawrence Erlbaum Associates.

[4] Main, M., Kaplan, N., & Cassidy, J. (1985). Security in infancy childhood, and adulthood: A move to the level of representation. *Monographs of the Society for Research in Child Development, 50*, Serial No. 209.

George, C. & West, M. (2001). The development and preliminary validation of a new measure of adult attachment: the adult attachment projective. *Attachment & Human Dev., 3*[1], 30-61.

Holmes, B.M. & Lyons-Ruth, K. (2006). The relationship questionnaire- Clinical Version RW-CV: Introducing a profoundly-distrustful attachment style. *Inf. Men. Health J., 27*[3], 310-325.

[5] Birnbaum, G.E., Orr, I., Mikulincer, M., Florian, V. (1997). When marriage breaks-up: does attachment contribute to coping and mental health? J Soc Pers Relat *14*:643-54.

[6] Fisher, HE (2006). *TED Talk:* Romantic Love.

[7] Porges, S.W. (2011). *The Polyvagal Theory: Neurophysiological foundations of emotions, attachment, communication, and self-regulation.* NY. WWNorton.

[8] Davis, D., Shaver, P.R., Vernon, M.L. (2003). Physical emotional and behavioral reactions to breaking up: the roles of genes, age, environmental involvements, and attachments style. *Pers. Soc. Psychol. Bull. 29:* 971- 884.

[9] Lucas, R.E. (2005). Time does not heal all wounds: a longitudinal study of reactions and adaptation to divorce. *Psychol. Sci. 16:* 945-50.

[10] Lee, L.A., Sbarra, D., Mason, A.E., Law RW (2011). Attachment anxiety verbal immediacy and blood pressure: Results from a lab analog study following marital separation. *Personal Relationships, 18,* 285-301.

[11] Childa, Y., Steptoe, A. (2010). Greater cardiovascular responses to lab mental stress are associated with poor subsequent cardiovascular risk status: A meta-analysis of prospective evidence. *Hypertension, 55,* 1026-32.

[12] Kiecolt-Glaser, J.K., Fisher, L.D., Ogrocki, P., Stout, J.C., Speicher CE, & Glaser R (1987). Marital quality, marital disruption and immune function. *Psychosomatic Medicine, 49,* 13-34.

[13] Holt-Lunstad, J., Smith, T.B., Layton, J.B. (2010). Social relationships and mortality risk: a meta-analytic review. PLoS Med 2010, 7: e1000316.

[14] Larson, G.M. & Sbarra, D.A. (2015). Participating in Research on Romantic Breakups Promotes Emotional Recovery via Changes in Self-Concept Clarity. *Social Psych & Pers Science* 1-8. DOI: 10.1177/1948550614563085 spps.sagepub.com.

[15] Weiss, R.S. (1975). *Marital Separation.* NY, NY, Basic Books.
Slotter, E.B., Gardner, W.L., Finkel, E.J. (2010). Who am I without you? The influence of romantic breakup on the self-concept. So. Psychol Personal Sci 36:147-160.

[16] Agnew, C.R., Van Lange, P.A.M., Rusbult, C.E. & Langston, C.A., (1998). Cognitive interdependence: Commitment and the mental representations of close relationships. *Personality & Social Psych.* 74:939–954.

[17] Sbarra, D.A. Hazan, C. (2008). Coregulation, dysregulation, and self-regulation: an integrative analysis and empirical agenda for understanding attachment, separation, loss, and recovery. *Pers Soc Psychol Rev*, 12:141-167.

[18] Hofer, M.A. (1984). Relationships as regulators: a psychobiologic perspective on bereavement. *Psychosom. Med.* 46:183-97.

Butler, E.A. & Randall, A.K. (2013). Emotional coregulation in close relationships. *Emotion Rev.* 5:202-210.

[19] Mason, A.E., Law, R.W., Bryan, A.E.B., Portly, R.M., Sbarra, D.A. (2012). Facing a break-up: electromyographic responses moderate self-concept recovery following a romantic separation. *Pers Relatsh* 19:551-568.

[20] Sbarra, D.A., Smith, H.L., & Mehl, M.R. (2012). When leaving your ex love yourself: Observational ratings of self-compassion predict the course of emotional recovery following marital separation. *Psych. Science, 23,* 261-9.

[21] Davis, D., Shaver, P.R., Vernon, M.L. (2003). Physical emotional and behavioral reactions to breaking up: the roles of genes, age, environmental involvements, and attachments style. *Pers. Soc. Psychol. Bull.* 29: 971-884.

[22] Nolen-Hoeksema, S., Wisco, B.E., & Lyubomirsky, S. (2008). Rethinking rumination. *Perspectives on Psychological Science,* 3:400-424.

[23] Kross, E., Gard, D., Deldin, P., Clifton, J., & Ayduk, O. (2012). "Asking why" from a distance: Its cognitive & emotional consequences for people with major depressive disorder. *J. Abnorm. Psychol.* 121: 559.

[24] Rye, M.S., Folck, C.D., Heim, T.A., Olszewski, B.T., Traina, E. (2004). Forgiveness of an ex-spouse: how does it relate to mental health following a divorce? *J Divorce Remarriage,* 41:31-51.

[25] Masi, C.M., Chen, H-Y, Hawkley, L.C., Cacioppo, J.T. (2011). A meta-analysis of interventions to reduce loneliness. *Pers Soc Psychol Rev.* 15:219-266.

[26] Sbarra, D.A., Boals, A., Mason, A.E., Larson, G.M., & Mehl, M.R., (2013). Expressive writing can impede emotional recovery following marital separation. *Clinical Psychological Science,* 1, 120-134.

[27] Beckes, L. & Coan, J.A. (2011). Social Baseline Theory: the role of social proximity in emotion & economy of action *Soc. Pers. Psychol. Compass;* 5: 976-88.

[28] Umberson, D. & Williams, K. (2005). Marital quality, health, and aging: Gender equity? *The Journal of Gerontology, Series B: Psychological Sciences & Social Sciences, 60* (Special Issue 2), S109–S113.

Waldinger, R.J. & Schulz, M.S. [9.15.16]. The Long Reach of Nurturing Family Environments: Links with Midlife Emotion-Regulatory Styles and Late-Life Security in Intimate Relationships, *Psychological Science* OnlineFirst as doi:10.1177/0956797616661556.

[29] Holt-Lunstad, J., Smith, T.B., & Layton, J.B. (2010). Social relationships and mortality risk: A meta-analytic review. *PLoS Medicine, 7*(7), Article e1000316. doi:10.1371/journal.pmed.1000316.

[30] Tatkin, S. (2014). PACT Training Manual, Module 3 p. 4.

[31] These guidelines come from Helen Fisher, PhD., talk at ICP in NYC 10/13/16.

Joy A. Dryer, Ph.D., wears four professional hats: a) psychologist clinician; b) educator, supervisor, and former adjunct associate professor; c) collaborative divorce coach, mediator, parent coordinator; and d) author and public speaker, integrating all the above.

For over 35 years, Dr. Dryer has been a licensed psychologist and certified psychoanalyst with a private psychology practice in Brooklyn Heights and Poughkeepsie, New York. Working with individuals, groups, and couples, she has an expertise with couples in both marriage therapy and pre-divorce counseling.

As an educator, Dr. Dryer was an adjunct associate professor in the psychology departments of New York University [Master's Program] and Brooklyn College. She continues to supervise graduate students. Organizationally, she is a member of two analytic institutes, NYU Post Doctoral Program and Westchester Center for Psychoanalytic Psychotherapy. She is president of the Hudson Valley Psychological Association.

As a divorce consultant, collaborative divorce coach, and mediator, Dr. Dryer is a member of the International Academy of Collaborative Professionals and the Hudson Valley collaborative divorce practice group, where she serves on the executive committee.

At times, when couples seek a separation/divorce consultation, she may have an opportunity to apply her advanced training in PACT [Psychobiologic Approach to Couples Therapy]. When a couple is available to explore, she has had success in challenging couples to think and to act clearly about the process of their separation/divorce decisions.

Dr. Dryer regularly writes and speaks publicly at both psychoanalytic and divorce conferences. She writes a monthly blog for *Huffington Post* and has a Twitter following @JoyDryerPhD. She is always interested in your feedback via jdryerphd@gmail.com.

Dr. Dryer's dissertation examined how integrating emotion and intellect enhanced creativity in children's play. She is still passionate about helping people enlist their creative "best selves" during therapy or during the difficult divorce process. She believes that teaching others, working in a team, and braiding together expertise from several fields searches out our values foundational to a meaningful life.

*Married parents are able to share responsibilities and lean on one another for help. One parent may work as the primary breadwinner while the other parent stays at home as the primary caregiver and household manager. Or, if both parents work, they likely share caregiving and household responsibilities. While the division may not be equal or as fair as one would hope, the help is still there as the couple works as a team toward their common goals.*

*But once a couple decides to divorce, each individual is forced to take on all responsibilities for his own household. This can be especially daunting when considering the new responsibilities with which he may not be comfortable.*

*Perhaps the most important transition that a divorcing parent makes is the transition from spouse to co-parent. On top of all of the new responsibilities, parents will need to reframe their relationship with one another. At least initially, children of divorce will need more from their parents as they go through this difficult transition. The most effective co-parents are flexible with one another and openly communicate about their children's needs. Despite living in separate households, they are able to make decisions together about their children and effectively and efficiently resolve conflicts. They are able to put their children first, in front of their own wants and needs.*

## THE TRANSITION FROM SPOUSE TO CO-PARENT:
### THE COLLABORATIVE DIVORCE TRANSFORMATIONAL EXPERIENCE
### BY LISA GABARDI, PH.D.

What if parents could not only get a legal divorce settlement but also get a roadmap for how to parent from two separate houses? How do parents create one of the most important partnerships in life, one to conduct the business of raising their children well, with someone with whom they could not maintain a personal partnership? Wouldn't it be nice to have a roadmap and guide for this process?

The collaborative divorce professional team, and specifically mental health coaches, can serve in this capacity. A coach can help parents build effective communication and conflict resolution skills as well as help manage the intense emotions and stress of divorce so that soon-to-be former spouses are able to effectively co-parent. Collaborative divorce professionals educate, model, and help parents experience a peaceful, non-adversarial, respectful way of handling conflict and making decisions. The collaborative process not only creates a divorce settlement but also sends parents on a path to becoming co-parents with new knowledge and experiences on how to handle their conflicts and make decisions on behalf of their children. They can use the structures and skills experienced in the collaborative divorce process as co-parents moving forward. In this way, the collaborative process is not only an alternative dispute resolution option for divorce settlement but also a transformational experience for parents that sets them on a path toward healing and in transition from spouses to strong co-parents.

## WHAT CHILDREN NEED FROM PARENTS DURING AND AFTER DIVORCE

Research informs us that key factors affecting children's adjustment to divorce include the child's temperament, parents' divorce adjustment and stress management, the quality of the parent-child relationship, and the effectiveness of and level of conflict in the co-parenting relationship. Aside from a child's own temperament, parents can help children adjust well to divorce when parents are coping well with the divorce, have a strong relationship with their child, and minimize conflict, cooperate, and coordinate as co-parents. That's a tall order during a divorce when stress is high and coping resources may be spread thin. Often, the other parent is a primary source of pain and stress. Collaborative divorce not only provides a non-adversarial settlement option, it also provides a structure and process that promotes beginning the process of healing and transitioning from spouses to co-parents. The coach offers support, education, new ideas and perspectives, and skill development. These roles facilitate emotion regulation, healing from loss, stress management, openness to flexible thinking and coming to agreement, communication skills, and conflict resolution skills.

## THE ESSENTIAL TASKS AND SKILLS
## OF AN EFFECTIVE CO-PARENTING RELATIONSHIP

### A New Relationship

One of the many necessary changes during a divorce involves parents no longer treating each other in the ways they did when they were married to each other. Parents must create new ways of interacting solely for the purpose of raising their children. In the transition from being spouses to co-parents, many aspects of the former relationship end, while the parenting aspect of the relationship continues in a somewhat different form. This can be an awkward and difficult process. It may feel strange and uncomfortable. But new interaction patterns as co-parents that are different and uncomfortable can be better than the comfortably familiar, unpleasant, and painful interaction patterns as spouses. Co-parents have different, more distant and formal boundaries than spouses. Effective co-parenting requires skills related to managing emotions, communication, conflict resolution, and creative problem-solving. Perhaps some of these skills were not present or were not effectively used in the parents' former relationship with each other. Effective co-parents are also able to separate their own feelings and needs from their children and remain child-focused in their co-parenting decision-making.

Creating new boundaries between co-parents serves several purposes. It serves to delineate a new and different relationship with a former spouse. In the new relationship, parents are more formal with each other and have new limits regarding what types of information they share with each other. The new limits of sharing information are solely about the children. New limits in their interactions can help the transition along and can contain some degree of conflict, as well as reduce slipping into familiar interaction patterns from the marriage that may not have been very effective. There may be a new, somewhat awkward formality and more business-like tone to interactions. While awkward, the formality and increased emotional distance serve a useful purpose. They reduce familiar old patterns from the marriage and signal a new relationship. Like the adage "good fences make good neighbors," the added limits to the relationship can help it function more smoothly.

To imagine more concretely new relationship boundaries, imagine co-parents as business partners. Business partners are bound together by an important common purpose and want their business to succeed. Co-parents are in the business of raising their children. It's a business, of course, that they want to be successful. Most parents want to raise healthy, well-adjusted children capable of functioning independently and well in adulthood. Like other businesses, in order to succeed, parents need to unite around their common purpose, interact in polite, respectful ways, share information necessary to the success of their children, and find creative solutions to problems. Successful business partners do not need to have a close personal or emotional relationship.

In order to interact in calm, respectful, and productive ways, parents must be able to manage their emotions. Parents do well to make personal time to address their feelings regarding the loss of the marriage and issues with their former spouse so that these feelings don't interfere with parenting interactions and decisions. An ability to identify emotional triggers and calm down is essential to productive interactions. Emotion control allows parents to be calm, respectful, and business-like. When parents control their emotions with each other, they can focus on problem-solving and solutions; when emotions drive parents' thoughts, words, and actions, parents become part of the problem.

With this model in mind, the new boundaries of the co-parenting relationship include: talking only about the children instead of sharing personal information and feelings; respecting the other parent's parenting time; honoring the terms of the parenting plan; being on time and reliable; respecting the other parent's home and property; and focusing on the present new parenting relationship rather than on the frustrations, disappointments, and hurts from the past.

## Planning, Problem-Solving, and Decision-Making

Parents make plans and decisions for and about their children daily, at both the micro and macro levels. Just as co-parents will live in separate residences after the divorce, they will also be making separate day-to-day parenting decisions. Respecting boundaries includes respecting each parent's separate and independent ability to make parenting decisions day-to-day. Effective co-parents also make decisions together and coordinate regarding bigger parenting issues. Decisions that may be shared and coordinated include: which child activities will be supported (financially and practically) together; bedtime; curfew; and privileges such as the ability to have and use electronics, cell phones, and automobiles. Planning regarding travel, academics, health, behavior, and activities, to name a few, requires sharing information, communication, and joint decision-making. Being able to continue to plan, make good decisions on behalf of your children, and effectively address the challenges of raising children well requires good communication, problem-solving, and conflict resolution skills.

## Communication and Conflict Resolution

Co-parenting well requires that parents learn to communicate in ways that are different and probably improved from their marital communication patterns. Effective communication is focused, calm, and respectful, and it facilitates sharing information, understanding points of view, and making decisions.

Routines and structure for sharing information and discussing topics are helpful. Parents can do this in person informally at transitions, over the phone, or via email. Parents' business is now just the shared children, so it's important for parents to keep the conversations focused on the children. It's equally important that parents avoid conversations about their past marriage and their personal lives. The more conflict between co-parents, the more structured and planned these meetings need to be. Follow-up emails that summarize any specific agreements and future plans can reduce misunderstanding. Some parents find it helpful to use shared electronic calendars or online scheduling and communication tools designed specifically for two-home families. It helps for both parents to be on email, phone, or other mail listings to be notified directly by the school, coaches, or other clubs about dates, times, and locations of events. Direct access to this information for each parent reduces additional communications between households and reduces the possibility of miscommunications. Automated systems for sharing information reduce opportunities for conflict. These structures can help contain conversations and keep them focused on information sharing and resolving specific issues related to the children. Some parents also find it helpful to have more structured and detailed meetings with each other a few times per year to review larger issues, coordinate calendars, and address parenting issues.

Parents are more likely to reach agreements and work together when they focus on their high-road parenting values and goals. For most co-parents, their shared purpose as "business partners" is to raise well-adjusted, capable children into adulthood. Parents often have similar end-goals but differ in how to reach the end-goal. An effective business partner practice is to selectively pick battles. Letting go of micro-management and looking for ways to solve problems without involving the other parent (e.g., Can you re-arrange your schedule? Can you purchase a duplicate item for your child to have at your home?) are potential ways to work together, independently, and resolve an issue for one's self before it becomes a problem. Parents who are able to consider the perspective of their child and separate their own needs and agendas from their child are also more likely to be able to work together rather than in opposition.

Parenting is challenging. No parent is perfect. Effective co-parents practice humility and the golden rule. With the exception of actual abuse or neglect, children benefit from two "good enough" parents in their lives. Parents reduce conflict when they consider how they would want to be treated. Parents who can think flexibly and step back and realize that their perspective regarding the children is not the only, nor is it the "right," point of view are more able to avoid blame and listen to their co-parent's opinion. Sharing viewpoints creates a climate of cooperation and the ability to explore creative solutions that work for everyone.

Practicing basic communication skills is essential to the ability to co-parent effectively. Awareness and management of tone of voice and nonverbal signals are key. Use of basic polite phrases such as "please," "thank you," and "I'm sorry" can go a long way toward repairing and rebuilding trust and respect. Listening is such an important and difficult skill to do well. So frequently parents are too busy justifying, making assumptions, blaming, avoiding, resisting responsibility, interrupting, and debating in order to forward their own point of view to truly listen to the other parent. The children ultimately lose when parents are unable to step outside of their own perspective. Of course, parents will not always agree. That's unrealistic! Married parents don't always agree on how to parent their children; neither do divorced parents.

When there is a disagreement, practicing calm, respectful communication skills; practicing listening skills; being open to new ideas; monitoring assumptions; asking questions; and focusing on shared interests and common goals for the children can help co-parents move toward generating options and creative solutions. Trying to see a situation through the child's eyes can help guide parents toward a decision that respects the needs of all members of the family and keeps the child's feelings and needs at the center. Parents can encourage cooperation by offering to be helpful to the other parent when making a request of them. Acknowledgement of inconvenience to the other parent and appreciation of their efforts to be helpful or meet requests builds good will and a climate of cooperation.

## How a Coach Can Help
## Parents Develop These Skills and Make the Transition

The collaborative divorce process is based upon transparency and respectful interaction. The safe container of the process can help build and repair trust between the parents. The coach supports, facilitates, and assists the parents in creating and maintaining an environment of trust and safety during the process. Trust and safety developed with the coach and in meetings can allow parents to begin healing from the trauma and loss of their marriage and the divorce. Trust is built not only with transparency and information sharing, but also by being accountable to the team, following through with homework, and reliably attending meetings. These co-parenting practices of openly sharing information, follow-through, and reliability can hopefully continue as part of forming strong co-parenting practices.

The coach supports and educates parents regarding emotion management, grief, and loss. The coach can help parents understand their own grief process and gain insight regarding how their grief may be impacting the divorce process and parenting. The coach can also help parents identify differences between them regarding how far along in the "experiencing loss and moving on" process each is and how that impacts their interactions. In coach meetings, parents can receive emotional support and guidance regarding emotion regulation and stress management strategies. A key role of the coach includes preparing parents for team meetings in which they may become upset or triggered and need to manage their emotions. Parents gain experience in these meetings learning to manage their emotions, take breaks, ask for what they need, and communicate calmly. This practice is essential to the ongoing interactions they will have as co-parents.

As already suggested, parents need guidance in creating new boundaries for a successful co-parenting relationship. The coach can help parents begin the process of separating their lives and understanding when they need to conduct business together versus separately. The child specialist can also help parents understand the needs of their children and parenting practices that will help their children. The child specialist role is especially suited to educate parents regarding child development, the effects of divorce on children, what children need, and what parents can do to help children and stabilize the family during and after divorce. The child specialist is the "voice of the child" in the process and helps parents understand their child's needs and consider a child-focused perspective moving forward. A process for parents to learn to shift from their own perspective to entertaining the feelings, views, and needs of their child is challenging and also a helpful way for parents to support their children, move off their own agendas, and potentially find common ground.

The structure of the collaborative process, which uses agendas and homework, can help contain parents as they work through issues. The coach helps parents prepare for these meetings and helps parents learn to create agendas and structure their own conversations. Improving communication and conflict resolution skills in order to effectively problem-solve and make good decisions on behalf of their children is central to the value of the collaborative divorce process. Parents learn new, effective ways (communication and conflict resolution skills) to discuss parenting issues as well as their different points of view and concerns. The coach helps parents practice new skills for communicating and resolving conflict. The coach may paraphrase or suggest a different way to communicate a parent's point of view that may encourage more receptivity from the other parent. The coach also models listening skills and asks clarifying questions to promote understanding. Finally, the coach helps a parent consider the other parent's perspective, have insight about how the parent may trigger the other parent, and how to use these insights to find new ways to interact.

A key role of all collaborative team members and especially the coach is to help parents identify their goals, create shared goals, brainstorm creative options, seek solutions, and ultimately come to agreements. The coach can help parents develop a mindset for reducing conflict and coming to agreements. The coach helps parents begin to develop the habit of moving from past to present and future focus, from blame to problem-solving, from positions to interests, from win-lose to win-win.

Another benefit of collaborative divorce is that parents are able to develop a parenting plan together with the help of a child specialist, coach, or both. A parenting plan that is developed together and with a child-centered goal is more likely to meet the unique needs of children and parents. Parenting plans that are created in this way tend to have more parent compliance and be more durable than a "cookie-cutter" plan or a plan decided solely by a third party. A child specialist can provide specific input on plans that fit the developmental and other specific needs of children. A good parenting plan can function as the operating procedures of the new boundaries, structure, and conflict resolution process parents agree to live by moving forward. The plan becomes the new "rules of the road" for effective parenting by which both parents agree to live. It is built upon the best practices parents have learned in the collaborative process, with the help of a child specialist and/or coach; and ultimately forged with the common bond parents share—the deep love and concern they have for their children and their desire to shield them from being harmed by the divorce.

## Collaborative Divorce:
## Beyond Settlement to Transformation

The alternative dispute resolution backbone of the collaborative divorce process combined with the added coaching of mental health professionals contributes to a transformational experience for parents. Parents leave the divorce process not only with a legal settlement, but also with new skills, tools, perspectives, structures, and ultimately a new and different relationship as co-parents. They have a detailed, specific parenting plan as their map and "rules of the road." With the assistance of a coach, they have practiced managing their emotions and have begun separating their lives and healing. Through the collaborative process, parents have learned a method for dispute resolution. This process for respectful communication and conflict resolution can be used as they move forward parenting their children from two homes.

Parents enter the collaborative process as spouses in pain and in conflict. With the support of the collaborative professionals and the process, parents emerge transformed by the process and transition into co-parents. They are equipped with tools to successfully negotiate the business of parenting. Parents can't afford and don't want the "business" of raising their children to fail. Thankfully, the collaborative divorce process supports parents in their goals to shield children from the harmful effects of divorce and raise them well, separately, together.

References:

Bonnell, Karen ARNP, MS & Gabardi, Lisa Ph.D. Impeccable Collaborative Outcomes: A Full Team Approach to Strong Co-Parenting Presentation at the IACP 17th Annual Networking and Educational Forum Las Vegas, NV October 29, 2016.

Bonnell, Karen ARNP, MS Co-Parent Coaching: The Next Page in the Collaborative Playbook, The Collaborative Review Fall 2015 Volume 15, Issue 2 Pages 5-7,26.

Lisa Gabardi, Ph.D., has over 25 years' experience helping individuals, couples, and families with their relationships, marriages, and divorces. Dr. Gabardi maintains a private practice in Beaverton, Oregon, providing psychotherapy, couples counseling, mediation, divorce consultation, and collaborative divorce coaching.

Dr. Gabardi earned her BA with distinction in psychology from the University of Delaware Honors Program. She received her Master's and Ph.D. in counseling psychology from Colorado State University. She first became interested in the field of divorce in graduate school, publishing research on the effects of divorce on young adults.

In addition to providing psychotherapy and marital counseling, Dr. Gabardi is trained as a mediator and as a collaborative divorce coach. She has specific training in the areas of conflict resolution, communication, negotiation, family systems theory, and grief/loss; all topics relevant to working with families going through divorce. Dr. Gabardi is also the author of *The Quick Guide to Co-Parenting After Divorce: Three Steps to Your Children's Healthy Adjustment*.

She is a member of Division 42 of the American Psychological Association, the Community for Psychologists in Independent Practice, the Oregon Psychological Association, the Oregon Mediation Association, the Association of Family and Conciliation Courts, the International Academy of Collaborative Professionals, and the Oregon Association of Collaborative Professionals.

In addition to this professional experience, Dr. Gabardi has been married and divorced, been a single parent, and has remarried. She understands the challenges firsthand of "keeping it together" while "coming apart." These professional and personal experiences add to her ability to offer compassionate understanding and hope along with expertise, delivered with warmth and humor.

Dr. Gabardi is passionate about helping people find a more peaceful and effective way to navigate divorce. She strongly believes that painful experiences offer opportunities for personal transformation.

*A parenting plan is the agreement between divorcing parents regarding how they will share time with, make decisions for, and financially support their children. Many courts have adopted parenting plan forms that they require parents to complete before granting a divorce. These forms require parents to decide on many issues that they probably wouldn't have realized were important if not for the forms.*

*In a litigated divorce, the judge decides the parenting plan, without really knowing the parties or how they tick. Or, a lawyer or mediator may help the parties draft their parenting plan. But while he may understand the legalities of the agreement, he may not realize the psychology driving the parents and their decisions.*

*In a collaborative divorce, a mental health professional assists parents in developing their parenting plans. Not only will the mental health professional better understand the clients' and children's limitations that might not make an agreement feasible, as well as decisions that will have a greater chance of success due to the clients' dispositions, but she will understand the developmental stages of children. This special knowledge and training will mean a better opportunity for success once the divorce is final.*

## THE LEGAL PARENTING PLAN, COURTS, COLLABORATIVE PRACTICE, AND CO-PARENTING MATTERS
### BY KAREN BONNELL, ARNP, MS

### A NOTE TO THE COURT:

This parenting plan was created by the parents through the collaborative (or mediation) process chosen by them for their divorce. In creating the

169

residential schedule, the parents have put the children first and have committed themselves to a healthy co-parenting relationship into the future.

The parents recognize that conflicts may arise in the co-parenting of their children, and each parent understands the steps required by this order to address those conflicts. Each parent agrees to approach dispute resolution in good faith, keeping the well-being of the children at the forefront.

Finally, the parents recognize that portions of this parenting plan are enforceable by the court and that other portions of this parenting plan are aspirational, designed to inform each parent of healthy parenting behavior to sustain a skillful co-parenting relationship.

The dilemma in all paradigm shifts is the often disjointed shift of various parts that make up the whole. As we move from an adversarial, court-driven model of divorce to a family-centered, self-determination collaborative model, we continue to bump up against the places where our new thinking and practice is *not quite supported* by our old structures. In other words, there are elements of our practice and paperwork where we're neither fish nor fowl. As a collaborative divorce and co-parent coach, I work with parents to think holistically about how they restructure their family. I encourage them to think about each other as co-parents, their children as the beneficiaries of their ongoing co-parenting relationship, and their parenting plan as the architecture of their two-home family. Nevertheless, I find the legal document lacking, and at times in opposition with, what co-parents want and need for post-divorce parenting success.

### SKILLFUL PARENTING PLANS ARE FOR CO-PARENTS— NOT FOR TWO COMPETING PARTIES, NOR FOR THE COURTS.

I love metaphors. There's a couple that stand out about the

importance and value of a well-written parenting plan. The idea that it's the *strategic plan for the successful business of the co-parenting relationship* certainly provides one apt description. For separating/divorcing parents, co-parenting isn't actually an option (unless one of them relinquishes parental rights). They *are* co-parents. The question is, "How skillful will they co-parent individually or as a co-parent pair?"

## SKILLFUL PARENTING PLANS PROVIDE GUIDANCE FOR HOW TO RESOLVE THE TENSION BETWEEN PARENTAL RIGHTS AND DOING WHAT'S *RIGHT FOR THE KIDS.*

A well-written parenting plan will contain the agreements that outline the residential time. It will also describe how decisions will be made solely or jointly and how conflicts will be addressed. Details abound. Specificity and legal language intend to make the organic and evolving nature of family life across two homes as *black and white* as possible to minimize conflict. Consequently, the parenting plan may also instigate the tension between parental rights (as codified in the plan) and doing what's right for children. In litigation, courts often settle the conflict between co-parents. In collaborative practice, the co-parent coach will more likely serve as a neutral mediator to help co-parents resolve the stressful discrepancy when the parenting plan says one thing, but it doesn't make sense to the parents or work for the children. A skillful parenting plan points co-parents through a conflict resolution process that reflects their best intentions and goals for their children.

## SKILLFUL PARENTING PLANS CONTAIN ANTICIPATED DIVORCE ADJUSTMENT AND DEVELOPMENTAL CHANGES ACROSS THE SPAN OF CHILDHOOD.

Perhaps another metaphor would be a car's maintenance manual. Check the manual index and every light, button, and warning system is listed on the page number assigned. However, if a parent has never driven this car or if he bought it during a very stressful point in life under duress, the actual impact of the information found on page three may be nothing other than frustrating. Who knew that splitting apart every Christmas Eve and Christmas Day by an exchange would feel differently three years after divorce? Now, having a complete Christmas celebration would mean the world, even if it means that next year the children would have the same complete holiday experience with their other parent. How can co-parents anticipate the impact of divorce adjustment on their parenting plan decisions when they've never been through anything like this before? For some, after their divorce adjustment, once the dust has settled and stability is in place, it's like reading the maintenance manual for a station wagon when post-divorce life is more like a sedan convertible!

### SKILLFUL PARENTING PLANS SIGNPOST OPTIONS AND GUIDING PRINCIPLES WHEN THE STRICT LEGAL TERMS OF THE AGREEMENT DON'T HELP.

And what about those unusual sounds or changes in how the car handles that don't have a name? Where do you turn then? There's nothing in the manual that helps. Parents often look at their parenting plan as they try to schedule a summer vacation and discover that what they intended to be a seven-overnight vacation absence from their children just became 12 when the regular residential schedule gets added back in. *Next gas station is 52 miles and the gauge is on empty*. That's how parents often feel. Kids suffer from the tension and fighting—the ongoing legacy of disrupted family life.

### SKILLFUL PARENTING PLANS DISRUPT THE OLD ADVERSARIAL THINKING AND PLANT SEEDS OF COOPERATION, COLLABORATION, AND CHILD-CENTERED PARENTING ACROSS RESIDENCES.

We'd like to think that parents have the skills and where-with-all to solve the unanticipated problems that arise in family life as they attempt to implement their parenting plans. Some do! Some put their parenting plan in a drawer and never look at it again. Some parents, no matter how skillfully written the plan, will fight about the meaning of the word "an" in the third line of the fourth provision. Chronic fighting over a parenting plan often reflects an unhealthy attachment or inability to let go, grieve, and move on. No amount of legalese makes *unhealthy* better.

I've described the two ends of a spectrum. The bulk of parents in the middle hope to take good care of their children but are at a loss. They are often overwhelmed with the emotional terrain of divorce and changes in the restructured family and/or may have never had the skills necessary to work together, resolve conflicts, and remain child-centered. For all those parents, a parenting plan is often the needed structure for understanding rights and responsibilities as well as the foundation for a functional child-centered co-parenting relationship. The plan becomes something on which to rely, to lean into, and to guide as needed.

### SKILLFUL PARENTING PLANS PROVIDE THE BACKBONE FOR SECURE, CONSTRUCTIVE, TWO-HOME FAMILY LIFE FOR CO-PARENTS *AND KIDS.*

From my nursing background, the metaphor that best describes a skillful parenting plan to parents is *the backbone of your children's two-home family.* The legal elements of the parenting plan—those that are structurally and legally defined and enforceable by the court (and hopefully that will never need to be tested in court) are the vertebrae—they are the "bones" of the parenting plan. The bones will be documented and described in explicit detail in the legal parenting plan, providing clarity, strength, and structure. Strong bones are essential.

However, a backbone doesn't function healthily and without pain unless there are other ingredients. The "soft tissue" between and around the bones is just as important because it allows for cushion, comfort, and muscular strength and support for the bones when faced with anything from gentle movement to heavy lifting. This soft tissue includes co-parenting protocols, guiding principles, and provisions. These are "soft" by their very nature and not necessarily legally enforceable in court. Yet, they are identifiable, describable, and important to preserving the health and function of the family backbone—preventing breakdown from stress, conflict, missed expectations, and lack of understanding.

173

## THE PARENTING PLAN:
## ONE PART LEGAL CONTRACT + ONE PART CO-PARENTING DOCUMENT?

Where's the focus and locus of control? As a divorce and co-parent coach, I'm often nudged by my attorney colleagues about including the soft tissue into a parenting plan with statements like, "That's not enforceable by the court." I nudge back with, "I know. But it's functional, helpful, and guides co-parents to succeed and to stay out of court." They push back, "There's not a box for that." I implore them to use their craft to find a way to provide parents with what they want to include and have crafted together for themselves—and to get the judge's signature. They nervously tread into this mist of the unenforceable.

Perhaps this conjoined attorney/mental health parenting plan process is best symbolized by Dr. Dolittle's fictitious unicorn-gazelle cross, the Pushmi-Pullyu. Together we attempt to move from the days of litigation and courts into the era of family-centered, collaborative divorce and strong post-divorce families while preserving the "bones" of a parenting plan.

Some of you may be thinking that the courts have actually stepped into this arena of the soft tissue by requiring parents to take a class as part of their parenting plan process and prior to submitting their legal document to the court. However, we also know that attending a four-hour class on a Friday afternoon holds no candle to designing and signing a parenting plan together that makes explicit *specific co-parenting commitments to one another and the children.*

### HOW DO WE KNOW IF THIS IS A BETTER APPROACH?

What does the research say? Don't know—no data. That's the thing about paradigm shifts—we haven't been approaching parenting plans like this long enough to test, research, blind study, and get results. Perhaps we'll have that data in 15 years (since research like this often lags eight to ten years behind the cultural/social change). For now, we'll need to use our best judgment, teamwork, and listen to our clients in those first two to five years post-decree.

## FACILITATING PARENTS FROM UPSET INTIMATE PARTNERS TO CONSTRUCTIVE CO-PARENTS AFFECTS THE NEXT GENERATION.

We know that approximately 50% of our families will go through consequential restructuring from one home with kids to two homes. We recognize that many parents want the self-determination and right to establish how they'll co-parent together while living apart. Through a well-structured parenting planning process, they will learn skills, anticipate conflicts, and build guiding principles that reflect their parenting values based on their love for and commitment to their children. We know that what's best for kids is two good-enough parents engaged and caring for their children. Ensuring that fathers are included and welcomed participants in the childrearing process benefits everyone in the family. These are not legal elements. These are the results of strong soft-tissue: the co-parent education and the skillful parenting plan.

## WHAT DO DRIVER'S EDUCATION, PHYSICAL THERAPY, AND CO-PARENT COACHING HAVE IN COMMON?

The process of helping parents work together to craft their parenting plan is a bit like driver's education. There's study and driving practice, study and driving practice, study and driving practice over time with an instructor—all the while building two-home family skills with increasing competency. For co-parents working with a coach, I often refer to this as developing a parenting plan on "training wheels," in which parents get to try on and try out schedules and co-parenting protocols and fine-tune their practices and protocols to best meet their needs through direct experience while still in their legal and family process where they have adequate support.

Physical therapy provides the metaphor for steps taken after a major restructuring of the family backbone from one home into two. The co-parents continue to exercises with on-going supervision as they re-strengthen the new backbone of their family. This is injury prevention/conflict management. In a skillful parenting plan, the need or usefulness of co-parent coaching is anticipated and built-in so that co-parents don't feel like failures nor wait until the health of the family system or its members is so compromised that a full recovery may be impossible. We anticipate and normalize needs and prescribe steps to avoid a trip to the hospital/courthouse.

## WHERE DO BEST PRACTICES AND IDEALS FIT WITH THE REALITY OF FAMILIES RESTRUCTURING AND PARENTS GOING THROUGH DIVORCE TODAY?

Necessity is the mother of invention. As we champion the rapid paradigm shift in family law from a legal-centric, court-driven, adversarial process to a family-centric, family systems process that supports stronger co-parenting options and keeps both parents involved and engaged in constructive ways with their children, we'll find new structures that support best practices. Our messaging to clients will change from our first encounter through our last. The cultural attitudes toward divorcing parents will change. Our goal is for children to retain their once in a lifetime childhood.

Restructuring families are best served by both legal and mental health professionals working in coordination. Together, we will devise methods to advise, support, educate, and provide families with options that are low cost, efficient, and effective. We will take care of the short-term legal restructuring and do what we can to impact the long-term stability and adjustment.

If we can't see a new future for family law, if we don't value something different, if we aren't motivated by the possibility to innovate and make families stronger, the status quo will prevail. Keep in mind, there will always be families so compromised by their own personality factors, addictions, violence, etc., that will need swift court intervention and skillful legal counsel to act and protect. There will be others who will never walk into our offices. *But for all those who do walk into our offices for support, let's be sure our support is as legally constructive and family-centric as possible!*

Karen Bonnell, ARNP, MS, is a board-certified clinical nurse specialist with over 30 years of experience working with parents. As a divorce and co-parent coach, Ms. Bonnell has dedicated her work to thoughtfully resolving conflicts one person, one couple, and one family at a time.

Ms. Bonnell has served on the board of King County Collaborative Law and was a founding member of the Collaborative Professionals of Washington. She is a member of the International Academy of Collaborative Professionals and the Academy of Professional Family Mediators. Ms. Bonnell is a regular presenter on topics related to divorce and co-parent coaching, as well as advanced communication skills.

Ms. Bonnell lives in the foothills of the Cascade Range outside Seattle. She values the lessons learned in the "school of hard knocks" in her experience of creating a two-home family before divorce coaching existed. Her two adult children are her everyday inspiration for the beauty of love, forgiveness, and trust in the capacity of family in all its forms.

*A mental health professional is the best person to help parents in developing their parenting plan. While a lawyer does not have the special training to understand the personality traits or disorders of divorcing spouses, mental health professionals do.*

*Mental health professionals will also better understand whether it may be beneficial or detrimental to ask a certain child's opinion about a parenting plan.*

*Rather than simply check boxes on a checklist form parenting plan, mental health professionals will customize the plan to meet the specific needs of the family. Every family is different, and so every parenting plan should be unique.*

*Mental health professionals will also educate the parents on co-parenting and communication skills that will help the clients as they negotiate their divorce, as they co-parent after the divorce, and with all of their relationships going forward.*

## Parenting Plan Development
## in the Collaborative Process
### By Jeremy Gaies, Psy.D. and Jim Morris, Ph.D.

The collaborative divorce movement rightfully prides itself on its family-friendliness and its attention to the needs of children. This chapter discusses parenting plan development in the collaborative process. We will address what the parenting plan is and who creates it, and we will identify the major content areas of an effective parenting plan. We will also explain why individualizing the plan to the needs of a family is important and how the process of creating a parenting plan can help the family long after the divorce process has ended.

A parenting plan serves as the blueprint for the parents' new co-parenting relationship. It describes how the parents will work together on behalf of their children. In addition, the plan serves as a safety net for when disputes arise. A good plan can set parents on the right course and be an invaluable safeguard for times of conflict. Parenting plans developed via collaboration can be designed to fit a family's unique circumstances. There are basic, long-distance, high-structured, and safety-focused plans, but all parenting plans cover certain elements.

Who develops the parenting plan? The parents. They (and their children) will be the ones who must live with the final product and will only be satisfied to the extent they believe it is their product. However, parents typically enter this process without much knowledge about parenting plans, and ending up with a product acceptable to both parents requires a great deal of creative thinking and facilitation by the professionals on the team.

There are collaborative processes in which the parenting plan is developed by the attorneys without the involvement of a mental health professional and, in some cases, with minimal participation of the spouses themselves. However, we believe that there is tremendous value in actively involving the parents. Ideally, the process can be guided by a mental health professional who is an expert in designing and writing parenting plans. The advantage here is that this professional can teach the parents about co-parenting along the way. Depending on the structure of the team, this function may be performed by a mental health professional who is the primary facilitator of the team process, by a pair of divorce coaches working together, or by a mental health professional who participates as a child specialist.

The use of checklist-style parenting plans or other approaches that forego customization and thorough discussion of options is, in our opinion, not reflective of the best that the collaborative process can offer families. The best co-parenting outcomes are achieved by two parents who work hard together to understand their children's needs and who put in the time and effort, with the help of experts, to systematically develop a child-friendly and thoughtful plan for parenting.

Most divorcing parents have a lot to learn about effective co-parenting. We have found that an excellent time to teach parents some of what they need to know is during the development of the parenting plan. The professional does not predetermine the plan; rather, he or she educates the parents about what needs to be considered and how to determine the appropriate level of specificity and structure. Most importantly, the professional facilitates the communication between the parents about what they each believe to be the best interest of their children. By identifying shared parenting goals, exploring timesharing options, and engaging in the drafting of a detailed and customized parenting plan, these parents can learn how to work together as a team for the sake of their children.

While it may appear to the casual observer that much of the work related to the parenting plan occurs off-line in the office of the mental health professional, away from the full team, that is just part of the process. It is essential that the full team has a common view of the process. If attorneys are not helping to set realistic expectations for the clients, the mental health professional will be left in a very difficult situation. And, once the mental health professional has taken the formal development of the plan as far as he or she can, it is important that the full team step in and see this work to completion.

There are times when the full professional team's involvement is essential in guiding the spouses toward a final agreement on the parenting plan. For example, the attorneys may need to help their respective clients accept the reality that one parent may not be able to work full-time to support both spouses and also have the children fifty percent of the time. The team might also assist with creative problem-solving when there is a dispute about the wording for decision-making or for how to divide time over the holidays. There are situations when six heads are better than one, two, or three, and a brief group discussion at a team meeting can be used to overcome an impasse.

The two primary elements of a parenting plan are decision-making and timesharing. Decision-making includes major decisions, day-to-day or routine decisions, and emergency decisions. The authority to make decisions may be shared by both parents (this is the most common approach), owned by just one parent, or divided between the parents with each parent responsible for making certain types of decisions.

Timesharing constitutes the largest part of the parenting plan for most families. This section of the parenting plan identifies the schedule that the parents will follow and when and how the children will be exchanged between the parents. A number of important factors affect the selection of the timesharing schedule and, in turn, the allocation of parenting time designated to each parent. These factors include the children's specific developmental needs, the parents' abilities to meet these needs given their work schedules, their availability, and their desire to spend time with their children, as well as numerous other factors.

In addition to these two primary elements, there are many other issues that need to be addressed, such as how the parents will share information about the children with one another, how often and in what way the parent who is not currently with the children will communicate with the children, and what obligations each parent has in terms of offering the other parent the opportunity to care for the children when a parent is unavailable. Other items may include rules for traveling with the children, a mechanism for school selection, agreements about childcare providers, and methods for handling disputes about the parenting plan itself.

There are a variety of considerations that are essential in developing a parenting plan. First, it is critical to identify the parents' interests regarding parenting and co-parenting. In other words, what is the goal that they are trying to achieve? In most cases, parents are quick to recognize that one of their interests is to create a plan that meets the needs of the children and fosters the best long-term outcome for the children. Creating such a plan requires awareness of the primary risk and protective factors for children of divorce, with the obvious goal of decreasing risk and increasing buffers against harm. This is one of the areas in which a knowledgeable mental health professional can be indispensable. Another factor is the need to devise a plan that addresses the level of parental conflict in the family, as families with higher levels of conflict require plans that minimize the opportunity for friction.

Yet another factor is the role of children's preferences. Some parents are more open than others to considering the children's wishes when it comes to timesharing, but this factor is worth exploring, especially for older children. It is important, however, that no matter the circumstances, children are never led to believe that it is up to them to make this decision. Even if the parents decide that the preferences of the children are the most significant factor, children should understand that while their preferences will be considered, the timesharing allocation and schedule is an adult decision. In the collaborative process, the children's preferences may be elucidated by the parents with the help of the team's mental health professional, by the children's individual counselors or therapists, or by a designated child specialist working with the collaborative team.

There are circumstances that necessitate more complex parenting plans. An example is when one parent lives or intends to live at a significant distance from the children. In this case, the timesharing schedule must balance the importance of having time with that parent with the challenges and costs of travel for the children and the parent(s). Another example is when a parent has limitations in his or her parenting capacity. These limitations may be due to mental health issues, alcohol or substance abuse problems, a history of abusing a child, or inadequate parenting skills due to a parent's personality or inexperience. One more example is when a child has special needs, such as a developmental disability, a medical illness, or a physical handicap. In such cases, the parenting plan must be carefully customized to ensure that the child's needs will be fully met even with the movement between two homes and with difficulties in communication between the parents. Finally, there is the serious and unfortunate circumstance in which a child resists or rejects a parent. In these cases, the parenting plan must address how that resistance or rejection will be addressed and how timesharing will be handled over time.

The actual drafting of the parenting plan in the collaborative process is typically completed by the mental health professional(s) in consultation with the parents and the other professionals on the team. In most cases, the attorneys' role is primarily to review the parenting plan as drafted and to offer suggestions for adjustments in wording so that the final document is legally sound.

Different collaborative teams use different approaches in regard to the signing of the parenting plan. Some teams arrange for the plan to be signed in a team meeting prior to the drafting of the marital settlement agreement. This can be helpful when there is an intent to lock in agreements about parenting before the resolution of all the financial matters. Other teams defer the signing of the parenting plan until the marital settlement agreement is also drafted and finalized so that both documents are signed at the same time. Whichever approach is used, it is our view that there is a benefit to having the parenting plan signed in the presence of the full team. Doing so lends a ceremonial aura to the act, which adds to the sense of shared agreement and the experience of closure for the parents.

No divorce is easy, pleasant, or fun. But given the options, we believe the collaborative process affords the best opportunity for spouses with children to experience their best possible divorce. One of the great advantages of the collaborative process is that it fully supports parents in creating a plan for co-parenting that best meets the needs of their children and that works for their family for the long run. The process also creates a forum that nurtures the development of a healthy co-parenting relationship even beyond the parenting plan itself. Both of these products—a well-constructed parenting plan and a healthy co-parenting relationship—are evidence of the great value that the collaborative divorce process brings to the families who choose this approach.

Jeremy Gaies, Psy.D., is a licensed psychologist and certified family mediator in private practice in Tampa, Florida.

Dr. Gaies graduated from Brown University with a degree in psychology and completed his doctoral studies in clinical psychology at Rutgers University. After serving as a clinical assistant professor at the University of South Florida, Dr. Gaies worked as a staff psychologist and as a clinical manager for a large managed care organization. He moved to full-time private practice in 1998, providing a full range of psychological services to children, adolescents, and adults, with a focus on couples and families.

Dr. Gaies' practice is currently devoted to the specialty area of divorce management. Dr. Gaies provides peacemaking interventions to families, primarily through his roles as a parenting coordinator, a co-parenting consultant, and a collaborative facilitator/coach in family law cases. In this latter role, Dr. Gaies coordinates the collaborative team in moving divorcing spouses to a mutually-agreeable final agreement for the benefit of both the parents and the children. Dr. Gaies participates on a number of local, state, and national committees advancing the collaborative movement. He is actively involved in the Tampa Bay Academy of Collaborative Professionals and Next Generation Divorce. He is a part of a five-member training team with Tampa Bay Collaborative Trainers, a group that offers introductory and advanced trainings nationally. Dr. Gaies has also served as a representative to the Florida Academy of Collaborative Professionals, as well as on committees for the International Academy of Collaborative Professionals.

Dr. Gaies is the co-author of *Mindful Co-parenting: A Child-Friendly Path through Divorce*, which is a concise, reader-friendly guide for parents who are considering or pursuing divorce. He conducts presentations nationally on the topic of co-parenting in divorce.

After four years at Florida State University where he majored in psychology, James ("Jim") B. Morris, Jr., Ph.D., worked for four years in a wilderness-based, residential program for troubled youth. Following eight years in the business world, he returned to working with children and families. He decided to pursue his Ph.D. in clinical psychology, which he earned from the University of South Florida in 1996. He completed his residency and a post-doctoral fellowship at the University of Virginia, where he subsequently served on the faculty.

Dr. Morris left UVA to work for a large organization that operated residential and community-based programs for children and their families. He served as the director of clinical services with this organization, which he loved, but after ten years, he realized the time had come to return to more direct services. In 2006, his long-term interest in forensic work, along with his passion for helping children and families, led to his development of a private practice in the Tampa Bay area that focused primarily on families who were involved with the family court system. He currently provides the following services: parenting plan evaluations, parenting coordination, litigation consultation, psychotherapy, and collaborative divorce.

Having witnessed the damage done by litigation, Dr. Morris was drawn to the healthier alternative of collaborative divorce. He actively seeks ways to educate the public about this option and regularly serves as a collaborative facilitator. Over the last decade, he has observed the positive impact of collaborative practice, not only for those families who choose this approach, but also for the professionals who work with these families. He knows the collaborative movement has already done much good, and he believes it will do even more good in the future. For more information about Dr. Morris, you can visit his website: www.jmorrisphd.com.

*Family Systems Theory suggests that individuals cannot be understood in isolation from one another. Instead, they are understood as a part of their family because the family is an emotional unit. So what happens when that family unit falls apart?*

*As an individual or relationship in the family changes, the other members of the family unit will also change. Escalated tensions exacerbate these processes and result in problems. Mental health professionals on collaborative teams help the divorcing spouses understand that they are not acting within a bubble. Rather, every action has consequences to those in their family unit.*

*While an attorney often only hears his client's side of the story and zealously advocates that side, the mental health practitioner understands how each family member's actions impact on the rest of the family, as well as how an individual's past experiences shape his views on what will happen and how he will act in the future. This understanding helps collaborative teams formulate strong settlement agreements by which the individuals will be able to abide. For this reason, collaborative clients have far fewer post-judgment issues.*

## FAMILY SYSTEMS THEORY:
### ACHIEVING ONE GOAL THROUGH
### A KALEIDOSCOPE OF PERSPECTIVES
### BY RANDY HELLER, PH.D., LMHC, LMFT

*Out beyond right and wrong, there is a field... I'll meet you there.*

~ Rumi

He says that she is constantly nagging, judging, and criticizing him. She says that nothing she ever did for him was good enough.

He blames her for the lack of intimacy and sex in their relationship, and she says that she could not have sex with someone who did not respect and appreciate her. He said that he could not be respectful of and appreciate someone who always put him down. He also said that after so many lies, he cannot trust anything she says or does.

She complains that he is too rough on the children, rigid and controlling like he is with her; and he says that she lets the children get away with everything. He sees her as irresponsible and unable to make any decisions. She states that is "because he never allowed me to." He is angry and aggressive, and she calls him emotionally abusive and insensitive. She is sad, and he says that she has been depressed for years. She calls him arrogant and dominant, and says she is victimized and intimidated by him. What's a collaborative facilitator to do with this? How will all of these details and descriptions impact the couple, the team, and the potential outcome of the collaborative divorce process?

I would imagine that these presenting issues are not unlike those of many couples who appear before you in your offices and have decided to divorce—one entity of the couple blaming the other for everything that has gone wrong in their marriage. He believes he is right, and she believes he is wrong! With this as a common denominator, the question becomes, how does a facilitator help this couple? In this type of conflict, with a couple experiencing fear, lost trust, and incompatible personality types, how does the facilitator help them come together in the midst of their differences to be transparent, communicate effectively, trust, resolve issues, and co-parent? Further, how does a facilitator help the couple *and* the team to manage all of the emotions in the room, while at the same time, help the professionals to regulate their own reactions to these dynamics? That is the focus of this chapter.

## COLLABORATION SEEN THROUGH A SYSTEMIC LENS

*A cloud masses, the sky darkens, leaves twist upward, and we know that it will rain. We also know the storm runoff will feed into groundwater miles away, and the sky will clear by tomorrow. All these events are distant in time and space, and yet they*

*are all connected within the same pattern. Each has
an influence on the rest, an influence that is usually
hidden from view. You can only understand the
system of a rainstorm by contemplating the whole,
not any individual part of the pattern.*

~ Senge, 2006[1]

Ideas of mutual influence, interconnectedness, and relationships are found throughout the Family Therapy literature. Gregory Bateson, an anthropologist, studied the ways in which systems are organized, the relationships between the various parts of a system, and the pattern of communication that flows within and between the parts of the system.[2] This inquiry led to the understanding that nothing happens in isolation, that each entity of the system impacts another, and that one part of the system cannot exist without the other. Furthermore, it explained how one cannot separate the part from the whole without considering the whole. According to Bateson, a change in one part will affect the whole and a change in the whole will affect the parts.

A commonly used example to explain this theory is that of a thermostat that adjusts according to the temperature in a room. The thermometer within the thermostat senses changes in the temperature in the room and responds according to an ideal temperature that has been previously set by a homeowner. The entire system (thermostat, thermometer, temperature, and homeowner) is interrelated and constantly communicating with each other.

To this point, Bateson emphasized the notion of feedback loops. He punctuated that change will only occur as alternative forms of positive and negative feedback are altered. In my estimation, therein lies the primary responsibility of the collaborative facilitator. As a facilitator, educated and trained as a family therapist and systems thinker, I perceive it as my role and responsibility to continually be mindful of the flow of information and the impact that it has on the changing structure of the entire system. Bateson and Webb agree that Collaborative Practice and Systems Theory share the same philosophy. They are based on the ideas of interconnectedness and relationship[3].

Bateson corroborated with other theorists as they began working with schizophrenics and their families studying their patterns of communication. Bateson's work contributed to this group's non-normative, non-pathologizing view of their clients, and the perspective that all behavior makes sense in context. The literature suggests that "in the light of communication and systems theory, the origins of problems were no longer sought intrapsychically, but in the interaction between people[4]."

The compilation of our life's experiences is what dictates that which we believe about people and circumstances and how we all move through the world. For example, if we have been betrayed, hurt, or mistreated, it is likely we might assume that everyone is untrustworthy and react very strongly to any indication of that from another. If we were impacted by a parent who was aggressive or controlling, we could experience an intense emotional response to someone who appears that way. We all come to the collaborative table with our own frame of reference, as well as our own triggers that impact how we respond to one another. Developing an awareness of those influences will allow us to manage our reactivity to them.

From my perspective, the only way we can assist people in coming together in the midst of their differences is to challenge our own assumptions and the way we think about others and their behavior. To do so, we must abandon our conventional beliefs about how we explain human behavior and how we determine right from wrong and truth from reality. When we can successfully do that, the feedback changes, the communication flows differently, the interactions change, and the outcome can change. This is a very difficult shift!

How many times have you sat at the collaborative table and heard things like, "He is a narcissist, and she is bipolar," "he is abusive, and she is the victim," or "he is histrionic," and "he is passive aggressive?" How are these labels useful? Conversely, what is the inherent danger in labeling people in this way? How does that impact the way in which we treat these people and interact with them? How does that perpetuate how they interact with one another? How do we as professionals propagate that?

Systems Theory is the interdisciplinary study of systems, with the goal of explaining principles that can be applied to *all types of systems* in all fields of research. Family Systems Theory is the application of Systems Theory to interactions between individuals and families. Different from Psychological Theory, which focuses primarily on the individual, Family Systems Theory enables people to think of issues (marital conflict, parent/child discord, anxiety, and depression) within context. It allows people to move away from blaming others toward recognizing that how they behave or act in a given circumstance contributes to the way in which others respond or react to that situation as well. Development of an understanding that nothing happens in isolation can enable a person to appreciate that a change in him may facilitate change in another or in a situation. This can reduce conflict between family members related to parenting time, co-parenting, and finances, as well as other challenges they may face during and beyond the divorce process. It is essential that professionals working with a family system comprehend the tenants of this theory in order to effectively understand how their interactions as professionals affect the systems with which they are involved. This allows everyone involved to attend to multiple perspectives simultaneously without labels, diagnoses, or blame while considering the needs and interests of the entire system and fostering harmony.

## A CASE SCENARIO—FACILITATING THE *SHIFT*

After many years of marital discord, including covert and overt conflict in front of the children due to poor communication, a lack of intimacy, struggles with extended family and friends, and allegations of infidelity and domestic violence, Bob and Carol decided to divorce. They were referred to me by their collaborative divorce attorneys, who informed me that there was no possible way for them to manage the intense conflict of this couple without the use of a facilitator. I decided to meet with them together in an attempt to identify the interaction patterns between them, the flow of information, and the responses and reactions that they were eliciting.

Bob appeared quite distressed over his situation and decision because he truly believed he would be married to Carol for the rest of his life. When they had their children Sarah and Sam, now 7 and 9 respectively, Bob reported that he and Carol "both experienced the joy of a having the family about which they had always dreamed."

Bob explained, "I don't know what went wrong, but it seems that she is not the same person that I married." He went on to say that, "In fact, she is so far from the person that I married that it is like I am married to a total stranger."

According to him, when they were first married, a significant part of the attraction for them came from their apparent shared attitudes and values, compatible personalities, general like-mindedness, and similar goals and hopes for the future and for the future of a family that they would create. Although there were differences in their family backgrounds and religious beliefs, as well as in the ways in which they were raised by their parents, early on in their relationship, they perceived that these differences allowed them to bring experiences to the relationship that would actually facilitate their growth and development as individuals, a couple, and eventually, parents to their own children.

Now, ten years later, it appeared the differences between them were creating a gap that was too wide. Everything from their dietary preferences and restrictions to their professional careers, handling of finances, choices of friends, interests in recreational activities, childrearing, religious beliefs, and even their attraction for one another and sexual desire was divergent. Although they had tried marriage counseling several times, it appeared to be to no avail. The more time that passed, the greater the level of conflict became, to the point that it was significantly affecting the children. Sarah was unable to sleep at night, her grades were suffering at school, and she was more withdrawn from her friends and social activities. Sam was acting out at school, getting into fights with his friends, not listening to his teachers, and being non-compliant and disrespectful both at school and at home. Given that both children had friends from other families whose parents had divorced, the children were continually talking to each other and their parents about whether "they would be divorced too."

In addition, life with the extended families had become even more of a strain. Bob, who was never really "in sync" with Carol's mother, had become increasingly estranged from her. According to Bob, Carol's mother was constantly putting him down in front of Carol and the children. He constantly felt as if she was influencing Carol and driving a wedge between them.

Carol had little to do with Bob's parents as they lived in another state, and she was never inclined to reach out to them or encourage the children to develop relationships with them, despite their efforts to the contrary. Now, it had gotten to the point where there were two camps—Bob's and Carol's. They were no longer that family they had set out to create. The children were even beginning to show signs of taking sides. They blamed Mom for calling the police and suggested that was why "Dad had to leave."

Bob believed himself to be the same man he was when they married. He perceived himself to be very traditional, to have deep family roots, to have a deep faith in God, and to identify with traditional male roles—husband is the head of the home, leader of the family, and role model for the children. He stated he was raised by great parents who instilled these old-fashioned values in him, and he was not about to change. He was proud of who he was and did not see any reason to alter that.

According to Bob, Carol was definitely not the girl he married. At the beginning of their relationship, Carol suggested that she just wanted to be a good wife and mother and not have a career. She was satisfied developing her yoga training so that she could be a part-time instructor while the children were in school and work a low-stress, easy job for extra money. She did not express any interest in having a professional career of her own or getting a college degree. They both agreed to this arrangement—Carol would stay at home and raise the children, just like Bob's mom and grandma had.

But, suddenly, Carol changed her religion to Buddhism and became a vegetarian. She wanted to continue working as a yoga instructor part-time and wanted to home-school the children.

Bob felt very strongly that the children should go to public school, as Carol was not qualified to teach them, and he would not agree to home-schooling. Also, Bob thought that since he earned the money in the family, he should either keep the family home or they should sell it; Carol should move out of the house and get her own apartment and a full-time job!

According to Carol, she acquiesced to everything Bob wanted because she believed in the idea of marriage and a family. Due to their "agreement," she stayed at home, took care of the children, and dismissed any thoughts of having a career; thus, becoming more and more dependent on Bob for financial support. She suggested that Bob controlled everything having to do with finances and that he dominated every decision that they made. Carol said he undermined her authority with the children and didn't help around the house because, as he put it, that was "her job."

Carol charged him with coming home from work angry and inattentive to her and the children. She was angry and resentful, feeling that she had missed out on many opportunities in life. She fantasized about a future where she would be free to pursue her goals and dreams, be respected for the person she is, and have a true "partner." She reported they didn't communicate anymore, could not solve problems, and had different ideas and values about most things.

She knew for a long time they were drifting apart, and yet she tried to make it work for the good of her family. They hadn't had an intimate relationship in many years as they were always in conflict. Carol had renewed a "friendship" with an old boyfriend from college, and Bob was "insanely jealous." They had several violent episodes over her interactions with this man.

In the midst of their dissension, the one thing both Bob and Carol shared was their concern for the wellbeing of their children. As the children were young, both parents had wondered how a divorce would affect them and what they should do about it. They didn't even know how to tell the children and had concerns about doing it properly so that the children would experience the least amount of trauma.

Carol had concerns that Bob had already tried to turn the children against her by suggesting that she was the one who caused all of the fights, had "left him for another," and wanted the divorce. Many of Bob's family members and friends told him to hire a "big gun" attorney who would protect his finances, make Carol change her lifestyle, and "win" him his case. Carol was told that she had "the right to remain in the lifestyle to which she was accustomed."

Neither knew which direction to take; they just wanted these circumstances to be over!

> *The only true wisdom is in knowing you know nothing.*
>
> ~ Socrates

## WHAT'S A FACILITATOR TO DO?

Let us now assess this couple. What is the *truth* in this situation? How do we decide? What is the basis for our decisions? What is the frame of reference we have that is underlying the decisions that we make about another's behavior? How do we *know* who or what is right? What are the potential different outcomes when we view these people from different perspectives? How will viewing them as individuals who we blame because of their individual pathology and aberrant behavior affect the way in which we respond to them, the way in which our responses to them affect the way in which others respond to them, and in turn, the way in which they respond to each other? Conversely, how will viewing them as a whole, and focusing on the relationship between them, open up more possibilities for change in the interactions between them and others and a change in the outcome?

In our pre-brief for the first full team collaborative conference, Carol's attorney described her "as the victim of a narcissistic, passive aggressive, and controlling husband." Bob's attorney described him as "a wounded and angry man scorned by his wife's infidelity and histrionic personality." I, in contrast to the lawyers' descriptions, described the dynamics between this couple as I observed them: their patterns of communication, body language, triggers, as well as the way in which they reacted and responded to each other. I also described the strength that they had in the way that they loved their children. I attempted to help the professional team understand how all of these behaviors made sense in context and how seeing only one side and believing they must protect their client from the other's "bad behavior" would only perpetuate an adversarial process. They seemed to understand.

When Bob and Carol arrived, the air was thick with tension. As we reviewed the collaborative participation agreement and discussed the expectations of conduct, Bob refused to look at his wife or her attorney. The tension increased. When Bob spoke, he did so as if his wife was not in the room. She slipped further and further into her chair and turned to her attorney for help. Within moments, Carol's attorney lashed out. She exclaimed that he "was not being collaborative," and demanded that he address both of them with respect."

I decided it was time for a break. In my attempt to attend to multiple perspectives simultaneously, I suggested a timeout in order to speak with Bob, Carol, and then the team. All agreed. What I came to discover was that Bob had just found out that Carol had spent the night with her "friend" prior to coming to this meeting. He said he "could not look at her." Carol said that she spent the night at a friend's house because they had a fight the night before, Bob "was aggressive in front of the children," and she "wanted to keep the peace." Who is right, and who is wrong? What is truth, and what is real? Although Bob appeared to be the aggressor and Carol the victim, which came first, and what followed? We cannot know, and it really does not matter.

However, as the facilitator, what *does* matter is the way in which we all respond to these circumstances in an effort to move forward. Helping each client understand the reality of the other's experience enabled them to have a modicum of compassion and to soften. They were then able to acknowledge their part in the creation of the conflict. The attorneys, who began by categorizing these people by their behavior, were able to begin to understand and acknowledge what was going on in the room, make fewer assumptions, and react differently. I was able to punctuate the reasons why they came to the collaborative table to begin with and the ways in which they loved their children and wanted to create a better outcome for them. We were able to continue.

The simplicity with which I describe this process does not fully depict the art that is required to accomplish this feat. The realization of this evolved understanding can only emerge out of an open mind, a willingness to see all points of view, and an acknowledgement of our own frame of reference that is perpetuating our behavior and that of others. A greater understanding of Family Systems Theory and its application can enable professionals to work more effectively with the diversity of the interconnected individuals of a system—all toward a common goal.

---

[1] Senge, P. M. (2006). *The fifth discipline: The art & practice of the learning organization* (2nd ed.). New York, NY: Doubleday/Currency.

[2] Bateson, G. (1972). *Steps to ecology of the mind.* Chicago, IL: University of Chicago Press.

[3] Webb, S. (2008). Collaborative Law: A practitioner's perspective on its history and current practice. *American Academy of Matrimonial Law,* 21, 155-169.

[4] Lawson, D. M., & Prevatt, F. F. (1999). *Casebook in family therapy.* Belmont, TN: Wadsworth Publishing Company.

Randy Heller, Ph.D., LMHC, LMFT, received her doctorate in family therapy from Nova Southeastern University. She has held multiple positions as an educator, exceptional student specialist, and family counselor for the Broward County School Board beginning in 1980.

She is now a licensed mental counselor, licensed marriage and family therapist, certified Supreme Court family mediator, qualified parenting coordinator, certified hypnotherapist, and founder and clinical director of The Family Network Collaborative Counseling Center for Positive Growth and Change, established in 1994.

Dr. Heller has had highly successful experiences working with individuals of all ages—parents, couples, stepfamilies, children of divorce, and students with educational, motivational, and behavioral challenges—facilitating change in their behavior, interactions, and relationships. She is a clinical member and approved supervisor of the American Association of Marriage and Family Therapists.

Dr. Heller has received specialized training in collaborative family practice. She is a member of the International Academy of Collaborative Professionals and the Association of Family and Conciliation Courts. Dr. Heller serves as a board member of the Florida Academy of Collaborative Professionals, vice president of the Collaborative Family Law Professionals of South Florida, and an active member of the research committee of the IACP.

Dr. Heller has researched and published her doctoral dissertation on competency and the role of the mental health counselor in collaborative family practice. She has also published an article in the Collaborative Review Research Edition, as well as three book chapters on collaborative practice. She has recently written the syllabus and teaches an elective course for graduate students in collaborative divorce at Nova Southeastern University in the department of family therapy. Dr. Heller has been awarded two concurrent grants from the IACP and is currently working in collaboration with MISSION UNITED/Legal Aid, Nova Southeastern University, and the Collaborative Family Law Professionals of South Florida to provide *pro bono* collaborative divorce services to veterans and their families.

*Our histories shape how we act in the future. Children who grow up in happy, healthy families typically find themselves in similar marriages. Parents who openly communicate with one another and with their children raise individuals who are able to do the same once they start their own families.*

*Unfortunately, the opposite is true, too. Parents who fight relentlessly in front of their children are unwittingly teaching their children to do the same in their own relationships. How do you stop this cycle?*

*Educating parents about healthy communication is key to helping them raise a healthier next generation. Although parents involved in a collaborative divorce are at the end of their relationship and may have already done years of damage, it is never too late to teach productive communication skills. These parents will have to co-parent after the divorce, and their children will benefit from the skills they learn through the collaborative process. The same cannot be said about litigation, which only promotes poor and hostile communication between the parents.*

*A collaborative divorce will teach parents, and inevitably their children, to be better communicators going forward.*

## WORDS MATTER
### BY KIM COSTELLO, PSY.D., LMHC

I was in high school when I finally discovered my place in the perfect family. My place was on the sofa watching television every afternoon, and the perfect family was the Ingalls of *Little House on the Prairie.*

*Little House* depicted the life and adventures of the Ingalls, a family of the 19th century American West, and I absolutely loved it. I loved how the Ingalls Family ate together every night and how the father actually took time to be with his children. I couldn't help but notice how Charles and Caroline, the parents, spoke to each other and cared for their children. The father and the mother possessed an incredible respect for one another, and I don't recall a single episode in which their fighting spiraled out-of-control or their argument ruined the family's dinner. I'd race to complete my homework every day after school so that I could be ready when *Little House* came on. I'd lie across our old cloth sofa and literally not move until the show ended, entranced by the portrait painted of a perfect, happy family.

My friends sometimes mocked me for my infatuation with *Little House*, but I didn't care. I couldn't help it; I was a romantic, and I cherished love stories and movies in which the family interacted together in harmony as in *Little House*. I believed that "happily ever after" had to be possible, and I'd found it in the Ingalls.

Not only were they a happy family but they often took people into their home who needed their support. I remember thinking how beautiful it was that the Ingalls threw open their doors to so many to help them heal through their love and kindness.

My own home was not the same. My parents would certainly welcome guests, but I always worried that, if I brought a friend home, she would not see the love and kindness I cherished in *Little House*. Would my parents pick a fight? Would my mom slam a door? Would my dad make some cutting remark? It was not a pleasant experience for me to have company over. I experienced gut-wrenching anxiety, waiting on pins and needles until it was time for them to leave. I feared I'd be embarrassed or, worse yet, that my friend would discover the secret with which I lived, the secret I myself discovered alone in our den at the end of an episode one evening. When the show was over, I recall feeling very sad and having an ache in my heart. I will never forget the sadness and awareness I felt in that moment. The reality of my family life hit me. "My parents don't love each other." Our family existed, but we weren't connected. There weren't any smiles at the dinner table, just elevated voices echoing against the decorated walls. No one ever laughed at my house.

My mom had a beauty salon in our home, and work was her easy escape from being with my father. My father worked a laborious job for the Department of Transportation. He started early, worked hard, and returned home to assist in all the household chores, but there was never any joy. I knew something was missing in my family, and I longed for an inner peace, a tranquil environment in which our family would interact positively and enjoy each other's comfort. I knew my brother wanted the same thing. He would often retreat to his room and play for endless hours with baseball cards. At a young age, he was able to master baseball statistics for all the Yankees. People thought he was a genius, but I knew that he memorized those statistics to escape from the tension and the heartache that was taking place one floor below his bedroom.

I knew my parents loved us, but their inability to work through their emotions and to communicate with each other was painful for both my brother and me. Their anger was like a cancer that spread through our family, and there was no way to stop this infectious disease from revealing its terminal devastation. I felt bad for my parents. I knew their life was not easy. They married young and had suffered the deaths of two of their children, one of whom died saving my life. They were hurting and angry, and they were each other's scapegoats. They would take all their uncomfortable feelings of anger, hurt, and guilt and displace and project those feelings on one another. They were a conduit for each other's pain and spewed their feelings daily in angry words and voices. My younger brother and I were their unfortunate audience. I believe deep in my heart that if they knew what they were doing to us, they would have made different choices.

In 1979, three things happened: I graduated from high school; my parents divorced; and I decided I'd never watch *Little House* again. I felt robbed of a healthy, happy home, and I didn't want to expose myself emotionally to an hour television show that was never going to become my reality. It was like being on a diet and going to eat at a buffet. You see all the food in front of you, but know you can't indulge. I came to the resolution that my family was never going to sit at a dinner table again. My parents couldn't even be in the same room with one another!

I am not sure if my parents ever went to counseling. I am not even sure that there was counseling in my little hometown in upstate New York. I just wished, as I grieved my parents' divorce, that someone could have taught them how to communicate with each other. Maybe they would not have hurt each other with such hateful words, and certainly, my brother and I would have learned better coping skills. We might've still had some family dynamic, maybe not like the Ingalls, but still intact. Instead, my brother and I are left with the jaded, painful memories of the hurtful words my parents threw at each other in their pain.

To this day, I remember those words, and I remember the devastation on their faces when they received those cruel words. Arundhati Roy said, "That's what careless words do. They make people love you a little less." That quote resonated with me all through my college years and still does in the later years of my life. My parents used careless words for years, and over time, they loved each other less and less.

At some point in my career as a counselor, I felt my purpose unfolding. It didn't happen overnight, but it did happen over time. One fall afternoon, a couple sat before me and told me they wanted to end their marriage. "We fight horribly, and our children see it because we are so angry and can't contain our emotions." My heart sank, not only for the couple but for their children too. My entire drive home from work that night, I felt the need to do more. I wanted to be a superhero with a cape that could save children from the pain of watching and experiencing hurtful words between their parents, words I myself had painfully endured years before.

Deepak Chopra teaches that "Passion is the free flow of natural emotional energy that leads us toward the fulfillment of our dreams, desire, and purpose in life." It was in this session that I began to understand my purpose and my desire. I wanted to teach people how to use their words to achieve healthier communication. My desire was defined by an unwavering commitment to helping families, but my dream began to expand as I saw in my own practice that almost all conflict within a relationship starts with words, with either painful words or with the lack of the right words. It was at this point when I had a heart-to-heart discussion with my husband about shifting the majority of my personal practice to conflict resolution counseling. I knew that I wanted to educate individuals how to change their words in order to change their outcomes in life and relationships. So, after decades of providing therapeutic intervention for individuals and families in times of marital transition, I wanted to assist parents and children in making it through the painful process of divorce through cooperation and open communication.

Through my training as a psychotherapist and experience as a counselor, I've found that it is possible to have happy personal and professional relationships by communicating effectively and mindfully. I've let go of wishing for perfection and "happily ever after" in my relationships, like the relationships I used to idolize in *Little House on the Prairie*. But, I fully believe that we can find peace in our lives and relationships if we work hard to interact positively with our loved ones, friends, and colleagues. I also believe that with support and education, divorcing parents can maintain peaceful communication for the sake of their children.

Soon after, I discovered I was not alone in my desire to find a healthier and more cooperative way to navigate the turbulent waters of divorce. Countless families have begun to catch on to the idea that divorce with dignity is possible through collaborative divorce. The results-driven growth of collaborative divorce can be seen every single day.

I believe wholeheartedly in the positive impact of this process and have shifted the entire focus of my practice to working with families in times of divorce. I now serve as a neutral mental health professional, parent coordinator, child specialist, and mediator for families in need. I recognize that every family is unique and that no two divorces are alike, and I provide services tailored to the singular needs of each family with which I work. My goal is always the same—to make the transition less painful by facilitating communication and cooperation when two people have decided they can't remain married.

I know personally how difficult it can be when you share your life with someone on a daily basis to be conscious of the words you use and how they impact your loved ones. Even as a professional who uses words daily to connect, heal, and help clients, I have to be mindful of how my specific words impact the people I love, especially my husband. On the rare occasion when my husband forgets to do something that was very important to me, I am guilty of bulldozing him with the, "You never . . . !" statement. Needless to say, it doesn't take long for my insensitive comment to derail everything. It sometimes takes me a few hours to come to my senses and realize that an apology is in order. In therapy sessions, we often teach communication skills, but rarely do we teach how specific words or statements can mar the relationship. There is a definite call for helping couples understand which words heal and which words inflame.

This chapter will help you understand the effects of your words and much more. You will discover the inspiring and devastating power of words, as well as the immense impact words can have on your brain, body, and health. Then, you will be let in on the secrets of mind awareness communication, to learn how to change your words to change your life. As you read, you will be on the path to more effective communication in your own life and helping clients achieve harmony in theirs.

Words influence everything. The vocabulary you use can have a resounding impact on your emotions, your thoughts, and your actions. Words are often internal representations of how people feel, and that is how words spoken by others are perceived by our brains. Our words become us and who others believe we are. The good news is that we have the power to instantly change the emotional dynamics of any situation and how we are perceived by choosing the appropriate words. We can choose the emotion behind our words, and we can also choose words that will create a successful outcome, something I call a "transformational vocabulary." Using a transformational vocabulary and positive emotionally-charged words can create a positive resolution.

The emotional impact of words stems from their connotation. The connotation, or feeling that words give off, can be placed on a spectrum that shows varying degrees of emotional intensity. The higher the emotional intensity, the higher the degree, or toughness, of the words expressing the emotion, and the greater emotional impact your words have on yourself and others. For instance, the feeling of anger can be expressed as being "upset," a word with low negative emotional intensity, or "enraged," at the other end of the spectrum, with high negative emotional intensity. When words with high emotional intensity are used, the recipients of those words can feel that emotional intensity and will react more intensely in response to whether your words are intensely positive or intensely negative. Take a moment to truly experience these next few words: resolution, love, ecstatic, devastated. You can see the varying impact that different words can have on us. We often make the mistake of using the wrong words to express ourselves, and that is where the hurt and misunderstanding, like my parents experienced, enters our lives.

Beyond impacting our emotions, words can also impact our brains. Each word you think or speak reverberates in your system and produces electrical impulses. These impulses affect your nervous and lymphatic systems, which get the brain involved. Positive words such as "peace" and "love" have been found to strengthen parts of the frontal lobes, promote cognitive functioning, propel motivational centers of the brain into action, and build resiliency. Hostile language can disrupt genes that play a part in the production of neurochemicals that protect us from stress. Even a single negative word can increase activity in the amygdala (the fear center of the brain) and release dozens of stress-producing hormones and neurotransmitters, which interrupt the functions of the brain.

The brain communicates directly and indirectly with all parts of the body, meaning that words that affect your brain go on to affect your body and health. For instance, the hormones and neurotransmitters produced by negative emotional words are pumped throughout our body and go on to affect our metabolisms. A negatively-oriented metabolism creates a disease state in the body for which our body works over time to compensate.

To illustrate this, researchers led by Janice Kiecolt-Glaser conducted a study at the Ohio State University's Institute for Behavioral Medicine Research. The study involved 42 married couples who made two 24-hour visits to the institute, separated by two months, so researchers could study the effect of positive and negative interactions on their levels of pro-inflammatory cytokines, proteins pertinent to healing and reducing inflammation. During their first visit, the couples were directed to focus on positive and supportive interactions. Each spouse was asked to talk for ten minutes about something he would like to change about himself, with the condition that it couldn't relate to the marriage itself. At the second visit, the researchers used the couple's pressure points to get them to argue for 30 minutes.

The researchers taped both the supportive and argumentative interactions and were able to distinguish between the distressed and non-distressed couples. The results showed that "stress is more important than we thought," as Kiecolt-Glaser explains. After argumentative interactions, blister wounds healed more slowly than after supportive interactions. The local level of cytokines, which promotes healing, was also higher for supportive couples. Couples with high baseline hostility had higher systemic levels of cytokines in their bodies the morning after an argument than couples with low baseline hostility. High levels of systemic cytokines are linked to cardiovascular disease, type 2 diabetes, arthritis, and some cancers. Therefore, emotionally intense words lead to body stress, which can lead to disease and even shorter lives.

Words can disease us and destroy us, emotionally and physically. But I want to remind all of you that words also have the power to heal. Effective, mindful communication is possible, and it is a practice I use in my own life, as well as suggest to all my clients. We can change our words, and through that, change our lives and the lives of others. We can make our marriages better by expressing our gratitude and our grievances to each other in loving ways. We can cooperate more effectively with our coworkers or co-parents by being actively aware of what we say and how we say it.

Dr. Andrew Newberg shares that,

> Language shapes our behavior and each word we use is imbued with multitudes of personal meaning. The right words spoken in the right way can bring us love, money and respect, while the wrong words—or even the right words spoken in the wrong way—can lead a country to war. We must carefully orchestrate our speech if we want to achieve our goals and bring our dreams to fruition.

Dr. Newberg's theory on how language shapes our behavior has now been integrated into my passion for communication. I travel across the U.S. speaking to others, teaching them the value of paying attention to their words, especially when dealing with individuals who are hurting. This practice of being completely conscious of one's words is what I refer to as "mind awareness communication."

So what exactly is mind awareness communication? Sally Kempton, an internationally recognized teacher of meditation and yoga philosophy, describes mindful communication as practicing right speech. She emphasizes that to "practice right speech it is essential to approach speaking as a form of yoga." I love this analogy because what comes to my mind is an evening at home when my husband and I decided we were going to start the practice of yoga. Slowly and carefully, we followed the DVD instructor into each pose. Eventually we reached Warrior Two. This particular pose requires intense concentration and focus, engaging your full body and mind. This is a very complicated task for someone like me, a multitasker who tries to get 90 minutes into every hour. Needless to say, right in the middle of this pose, I heard my phone ding with a new text. I tried to hold the pose and simultaneously reach for my phone, but as you can imagine, that that did not work out so well. My Warrior Two pose fell apart as I did. I realized in that moment that it is impossible to be mindful and multitask at the same time, and the same goes for practicing mindful speech. One must be focused and fully engaged to communicate with mind awareness.

According to Sally, the first stage in speech yoga or mind awareness communication is to become fully aware of the words you say. She recommends that you begin this exercise by spending a day eavesdropping on yourself—ideally, without activating your inner critic. It is important for each of us to notice our choice of words and the tone we use to say those words. This is an exercise in awareness. Eavesdropping on ourselves allows us to feel the "emotional residue" that our words create and how we feel after certain remarks.

The second stage is to understand that the yoga of speech is a type of self-inquiry in which we draw awareness to our words and what we are saying. You ask yourself, "Why do I say what I say? What emotions am I holding deep inside that may burst forth as lies, sarcasm, or euphemisms? Am I truly saying what I mean? How do my words affect others?" Sally encourages us to ask these specific questions so that we may become cognizant of any repressed emotional conflicts that lie beneath our speech. When you find yourself whining or speaking cruelly or just chattering to chatter, this may be an indication of underlying issues. She emphasizes the importance of owning and healing those issues. Sally believes that,

> Trying to speak from an authentic state of higher awareness without having done that healing is like building your house on a swamp. The underground water will eventually flood your basement, and your disowned pain will inevitably leak out through your words.

The example of comparing speech to yoga is brilliant. Yoga is a practice in which the more awareness, concentration, and commitment you have, the better your poses become. Communication is the same. The more you become aware of your words and commit to communicating positively, the better your conversation and life will become.

Awareness and mindfulness in communication are also beautifully articulated by Suzanne Stevens in her article, *Mindful Communication*. In this article, Suzanne shares how her mindful communication practice started out of her own struggles with multiple sclerosis. The disease greatly affected her ability to speak clearly, slurring her words until she was virtually indecipherable. She met frequently with a speech therapist to improve her diction and pronunciation. But what really changed Suzanne's life was beginning her practice of mindful speech. She practiced diligently in every encounter, and after several months of being completely attuned to her own words, she realized that she "spewed lots of needless things." Suzanne decided to give herself more time to construct her thoughts into words to get to the meat of what she actually wanted to express to others. She learned to listen more to others, to respond to them more appropriately without throwing out words to sound smart or feel included. Suzanne's story is an example of where being mindfully aware of how you communicate can make all the difference in your life.

Mindful awareness communication is not only practiced by individuals but is also one of the most useful practices for advertisers. It has even been used in the marketing of fish. One of my favorite dishes of all time is Chilean sea bass. I absolutely love this fish in all its tenderness and savor every single bite. However, if I had seen the menu back in 1977, I am not sure I could have been persuaded to even order it. Back then, it was called Patagonian toothfish! Chilean sea bass rolls off the tongue. It sounds inviting, pleasurable, and palatable. Patagonian toothfish sounds like a mouthful (no pun intended), like it would bite you back if you attempted to eat it. Not very appetizing. After marketing gurus decided to reinvent the name of the Patagonian toothfish into Chilean sea bass, it began selling all over the world. Becoming consciously aware of how words impact even the digestive system is just another reason to be aware of the meaning of the words we choose.

In my presentation, "Oops, I Meant to Say," on why words matter, I have a YouTube video I play of a blind homeless man sitting on a piece of cardboard asking for money. He has a small jar in front of him and a little cardboard sign that reads "I'm Blind. Please Help." As the poor, blind man sits with his jar and sign exposed, people continue to pass him by with little regard to his presence or his sign. Then, out of nowhere, a woman finally stops before him. She reaches for his sign, flips it over, and on the blank side writes, "It is a beautiful day, I wish I could see it." This transformation of words miraculously changes the outcome for the elderly gentleman. When people read the sign, they begin contributing money right and left. The reason they decided to help was because the words now had meaning. People could relate and feel what this man was missing by being blind. When we mindfully speak, we connect. This video depicts how our mindful choice of words can impact not only ourselves but others as well.

Now that you know the power and importance of words, as well as how to mindfully communicate, you'll realize that when you change your words, you can change your life. You have the power to use words to your advantage and to the advantage of others in any collaboration session, for words are stronger than they seem. They can make or break any session, any conversation, and any relationship.

As a young woman witnessing my parents' painful divorce in between idyllic episodes of *Little House on the Prairie*, I didn't know that a happy medium between those two relationship examples could exist. But today, I have created it with my husband in our marriage by focusing wholeheartedly on communicating effectively from a loving place. My experience and education as a counselor taught me the importance of words, and I was able to bring that home with me to make the strongest relationship I could. We try to speak as mindfully as possible to each other and recognize that our words can hurt, but also heal. We're not perfect. We get it wrong sometimes. But then, with our words and our actions, we have the power to make it right again.

In your own career as a collaborative professional, and your own life as a spouse, parent, sibling, child, and friend, don't underestimate the power of your words. Use them to create the career and the relationships that you've always wanted. Let your words guide you to success and happiness.

Kim E. Costello, Psy.D., LMHC, has over 20 years of experience as a therapist and counselor. Her experience and training led her to found The Costello Center with her husband Frank Costello in 2006, a comprehensive counseling and academic assistance center serving the greater Tampa Bay area.

Dr. Costello is a psychotherapist, Board Certified Counselor, Licensed Mental Health Counselor, Florida Supreme Court Mediator, Certified Christian Marriage and Family Therapist, Parenting Coordinator, and Neutral Mental Health Facilitator trained in the most current models for family mediation and collaborative law.

She received her master's degree from Norwich University and a Doctorate in Christian Counseling Psychology from Carolina University of Theology. She is a member of the American Board of Professional Counselors, the American Psychotherapy Association, the Association of Family and Conciliation Courts, and the International Association of Collaborative Professionals.

Conflict resolution counseling has always been an important component of Dr. Costello's practice. After decades of providing therapeutic intervention for individuals and families in times of marital transition, she came to believe that there is a better way for parents and children to navigate through the painful process of divorce. Through extensive training and professional development, Dr. Costello has gained a unique perspective and expertise in the area of conflict resolution therapy. She believes so strongly in the positive impact of this process that she has shifted the entire focus of her practice in order to more fully dedicate herself to her work with families in times of divorce.

Her innovative method for collaborative divorce has grown as families have realized that divorce without despair is possible. To this end, she is trained in the best methods for family mediation and collaborative law and serves as a neutral mental health facilitator, parenting coordinator, child specialist, and/or mediator for families in need.

*Collaborative teams work most efficiently and effectively when they utilize the established protocols developed in their community. Protocols prescribe the correct etiquette and procedure that the collaborative team should follow.*

*Because collaborative teams involve professionals from different fields of expertise who may be used to operating in ways that conflict with the ideals of the collaborative process, established collaborative protocols are especially important to ensure that the team works together cohesively. The protocols help professionals as they make the paradigm shift to the collaborative method. If a professional has difficulty making this shift, the team can point the professional to the protocols and guide the professional as to how his behavior conflicted with the established protocol.*

*The collaborative team is just that—a team. Protocols allow the team to work synergistically so that clients are able to meet their goals in a way that considers the families' best interests.*

## THE PEACEFUL POWER OF THE FULL TEAM
## USING ESTABLISHED PROTOCOLS
### BY ELLIE IZZO, PH.D., LPC AND
### VICKI CARPEL MILLER, BSN, MS, LMFT

Little six-year-old Robert sits on the floor by the low table in the child specialist's office, carefully choosing crayons and chatting with her as he begins her requested task to draw her a picture of a house. Robert frowns, and she becomes quite confused as he quickly completes the picture and hands it to her.

She holds it up and remarks, "Robert, tell me about this picture."

He whispers, "I drew a boat. I don't want to draw a house." He looks at her squarely in the eyes and continues, "My dad cries all the time and says my mom is trying to make him leave our house because of the divorce. He says everyone will have to leave the house. He says there is no more money for a house. I am *not* going to draw a house."

Yikes! After several decades as mental health professionals and over a decade as coaches in collaborative divorce, it still never fails to amaze us when we experience the sadness and anxiety of children of divorce. When the child specialist on this collaborative divorce case shared this innocent child's picture with his parents and their coaches, the parents were shocked. They were shocked at the picture of the boat and how Robert placed it on the page in very heavily lined, dark, stormy waters. They became quickly motivated to find ways to stop power-struggling over what they perceived as their failing finances. They simultaneously got back to their commonly held value, the wellbeing of their son.

The child specialist was the turning point in this difficult collaborative case when, as the voice of their child, she unified the parents.

The collaborative divorce process truly exemplifies the saying that "the whole is greater than the sum of its parts." The professionals build upon the strengths and expertise inherent in all the various parts of the team, influencing each other toward the greater good. Without the benefit of the child specialist and the rapport established between both clients through their work with their coaches on this case, the parents would have likely continued bickering about finances and parenting time. They would have brought in a myriad of outside professionals, spent time, money, and energy with warring opinions leading nowhere. They would be at risk to begin believing that they were incapable of finding acceptable solutions for their child within themselves. With the benefit of team input, and particularly the expertise of their coaches, they were able to effectively communicate together and refocus their efforts toward resolution for the good of their child.

Honestly, we think things have gotten even harder for children of divorce after the most recent recession. Kids used to be scared about their parents, their stuff, their schools, and their rooms in the face of divorce. Now we see kids, along with their divorcing parents, fretting more and more about money and the financial challenges of two-household families. As collaborative divorce coaches, we worry about these transitioning families and believe now, more than ever, that collaborative divorce is the necessary option for this population. Collaboration requires an attorney's highest and best use of skill, talent, and experience. It is the collective abilities of all professionals that greatly enhance our ability to produce better client-centered results.

Collaborative divorce, a full-team model of collaboratively trained professionals (two lawyers, two coaches, one child specialist, and one neutral financial specialist), addresses all the dimensions of divorce and helps today's financially weakened families transition peacefully, putting the needs of their kids at the forefront. It has historically never been the cheapest divorce, and it has never been the most expensive, but it has always provided an incredible value for the family in flux. Clients select all their team members at the inception of the case, sign an agreement to resolve their issues out of court, and proceed in a milieu of security, education, and guidance.

In today's world, how can fiscally struggling, divorcing parents afford to pay all the people on a collaborative divorce team? Overall, a full team of professionals who serve to address the necessary conversations, the needs of the children, and the financial wellbeing of the family actually streamlines the divorce process. And now, with our new streamlined protocols for collaborative divorce, family lawyers, mental health professionals, and financial professionals trained in collaboration can offer this service to their clients with efficacy and confidence. The financially secure, as well as the economically stressed, divorcing couple can now use the peaceful power of the full team to help their kids while they help themselves to reorganize, redefine their relationship, and regain control over their finances.

Why do collaborative divorce teams need protocols? How do they help? Protocols provide predictability, reliability, and consistency that promote cohesiveness and confidence in the full team process. Each professional is on the same path, understanding and implementing the same procedures, helping the clients to know exactly what to expect and when. The team follows the same path to reach desirable outcomes for the divorcing family with minimal detours, if any.

When lawyers, mental health professionals, and financial professionals are trained to work together synergistically as a team, they can directly and efficiently guide, coach, and educate the clients. It is imperative for professionals to participate and train in order to understand and assimilate the rationale for the protocols. The clients then learn this same procedure from all of their team members. As the adage reminds us, "If three or more people give you the same feedback, it is important to take it seriously." As a result, the clients follow the protocols, stay directly on course, and quickly reach outcomes with which they both can live and which are in the best interests of their transitioning family. The professionals leave the process satisfied, energized, and feeling positive about their work.

Are there some professionals who can pose challenges to the process or the protocols? Are there some who begin to advocate for their clients, put up barriers to resolution, and revert to more traditional litigating techniques? Of course. Old habits die hard. If one professional is not on the same page as the rest of their team, the team itself will work with that professional to assist them in returning to the collaborative divorce protocols in which they were trained. If left unchecked, this professional's behavior can run amok. The process then can completely derail and go sideways. The professionals may start to resort to more conventional adversarial interventions. When this happens, although infrequently, the professionals will commonly ask the divorcing couple to leave the meeting so they can participate in the necessary and difficult conversation they need to have to get back to the protocols back on track for the couple.

For each meeting scheduled, the clients are thoroughly prepared within their team to skillfully communicate with each other and resolve their divorce as they set their sights for a brighter future. Children who witness their parents approach divorce in this capable, confident, and hopeful way are less anxious, less sad, and more resilient. Don't you think every child of divorce needs this type of experience? We sure do.

Imagine if all the professionals working on a divorce spoke

openly about the issues facing the couple. If there were no hidden agendas or materials missing, would the couple have a better chance at resolving the challenges they face with transparency, honesty, and direct communication? With all professionals on the same path, expecting the same behavior and level of participation from their clients, clients choose to step up and accept the guidance they require while navigating through the "fog" of divorce.

The financial specialist is the only true neutral and will gather the financial information. She will also prepare the clients and the professional team for the full team meeting where the division of assets and debts is addressed. The less informed spouse will be brought to an efficient level of financial knowledge, empowering him to participate without fear, ask pertinent questions, and confidently make informed decisions.

The child specialist will speak with the children and relate key information to the parents with the coaches present to ensure they understand the specific challenges their children are facing. They can then make informed decisions about their children and their co-parenting structure.

The coaches, one for each parent in many jurisdictions, help the clients privately navigate through their intense negative feelings and worries. They help the clients to formulate healthy communications so they can be heard by one another and move through this difficult transition with skills to last a lifetime—because they will share their children for a lifetime.

Collaborative lawyers are trained to provide the clients with a container, a safe space to explore options for their future. They are not promising any outcomes, nor are they giving legal information without the other client present, so there are no surprises that might hijack the process. Collaborative lawyers address the legal challenges by encouraging brainstorming of options while providing information for legal sufficiency. They do not strategize to "get the most they possibly can" for their client. Because of this shift, a couple and their team are able to see the big picture as the household is being restructured.

When clients seek information about divorce, the collaborative professional team creates an environment of safety for divorcing couples in a stressful time. The team is uniquely qualified to address the emotional, financial, and legal safety zones required in collaborative divorce. In traditional litigation, divorcing clients use their lawyers to avoid facing difficult or necessary situations or conversations that when addressed in collaboration, no longer have the stigma or negative long-term effect they feared. Divorcing clients who distract themselves by any number of behaviors only delay the inevitable: they are going to be divorced. The choice becomes whether to actively participate in decisions about their lives or surrender their power and let someone else decide their future.

If we, as professionals, recognize that divorce is anxiety-producing and will likely create an anxious response, we will dialogue with our clients about how continuing in the anxious fight, flight, or freeze response will, in due course, negatively impact their futures. With the support, assistance, and expertise of each collaborative team member, the clients can make a deliberate choice to walk into the things they fear most, and ultimately, walk out the other side with guidance for a better understanding and education on how to communicate effectively for informed decision-making. They emerge with a feeling of confidence for having faced the issues head on, a final agreement they themselves created, and pride for choosing to walk the path through divorce with respect and dignity. When the anxiety recedes, and it always does, collaborative clients have a noticeably more positive outcome, a healthy divorce legacy for their children, and a brighter future.

Ellie Izzo, Ph.D., LPC, is co-founder and core trainer with the Collaborative Divorce Institute and the Vicarious Trauma Institute. Dr. Izzo serves as a collaborative divorce trainer, divorce coach, child specialist and/or team manager.

Dr. Izzo developed the Rapid Advance Process in 1990, a standardized five-step model for building neural pathways to higher thinking, which was originally presented at the American Counseling Association convention in Atlanta in 1997 and again in Honolulu in 2008. The Rapid Advance Process is now widely used to alleviate trauma and stress.

Dr. Izzo presents for numerous conferences and conventions. She hosted a call-in radio show in Phoenix and served as self-help editor for a nationally syndicated trade magazine.

Dr. Izzo is a member of the American Psychological Association, the American Counseling Association, the American Mental Health Counselors Association, International Academy of Collaborative Professionals, and Collaborative Divorce Professionals of Arizona (board member-at-large). Dr. Izzo is co-director of Arizona Collaborative Coaching Services, Vicarious Trauma Institute, and the Collaborative Divorce Institute. Her offices are located in Scottsdale, Arizona.

Vicki Carpel Miller, BSN, MS, LMFT, is co-founder of, and a core trainer with, the Collaborative Divorce Team Trainings, Collaborative Divorce Institute, and the Vicarious Trauma Institute, introducing the Rapid Advance Process for building higher thinking skills. She is co-author of *Second-Hand Shock: Surviving and Overcoming Vicarious Trauma* and *The Second-Hand Shock Workbook, Just Stop Eating That, Just Stop Picking Losers*, and *Just Stop Doing That.*

Ms. Miller is the co-founder of Collaborative Divorce Professionals of Arizona and functions as a divorce coach, child specialist, and/or case manager in collaborative divorce files. She has been training lawyers, mental health professionals, and financial professionals in the full team model of interdisciplinary collaborative divorce for well over a decade throughout the United States, Canada, and Australia. She was instrumental in designing the full team and streamlined protocols for collaborative practice.

Ms. Miller is a past board member and current professional member of the International Academy of Collaborative Professionals (IACP) and served on several committees including standards, core institute, forum planning, and the original advisory council on training and practice to the IACP. She is a clinical member of the American Association for Marriage and Family Therapists and the Association of Family and Conciliation Courts. She is an advanced practitioner in mediation. Ms. Miller has received advanced training in family mediation, narrative mediation, interest-based negotiation, high conflict personalities, collaborative family law, collaborative law in trusts and estates, and collaborative divorce interdisciplinary team practice. She has designed curriculum for introductory and advanced collaborative trainings, as well as trained the trainers in full team collaborative divorce.

www.ingramcontent.com/pod-product-compliance
Lightning Source LLC
Chambersburg PA
CBHW052125270326
41930CB00012B/2764